HORSES
breeds, cultures, traditions

WHITE STAR PUBLISHERS

Contents

TEXT BY SUSANNA COTTICA AND LUCA PAPARELLI

PROJECT EDITOR VALERIA MANFERTO DE FABIANIS

EDITORIAL COORDINATION VALENTINA GIAMMARINARO AND FEDERICA ROMAGNOLI

GRAPHIC DESIGN STEFANIA COSTANZO

Introduction

Nature and man are two fundamental factors in the history of the horse. They have acted both indirectly, as in the case of changes induced by the environment in which horses have lived for centuries, and directly, as in the intervention of the first breeders who, after taming the horse, contributed significantly to the formation of the various breeds.

The term "breed" means a group of individuals with distinctive well-defined hereditary features. Today there are many breeds of horses, some of which are very similar to each other while others have distinctive features. Although they followed a different evolutionary line, all are descended from a single ancestor, the *Eohippus*, which lived 60 million years ago, during the Cenozoic Era and, more precisely, the Eocene epoch. The *Eohippus* had dimensions similar to those of a fox and was about 30 cm high at the withers. It had four toes on each forefoot and three toes on each hind foot, thick toenails, and pads under each of its webbed toes. With these physical characteristics, this animal that fed on leaves and stems could move easily in its natural habitat of swampy forests.

Between the *Eohippus* and the *Equus caballus*, the modern horse, various evolutionary transitions and changes took place, due to changes in the animal's habitat. Over the millennia, with the evolution of climate and the natural environment, and in particular as a result of developments that led to the formation of large grassy prairies, even the horse underwent a significant evolution, resulting in major changes in its physical characteristics.

These changes culminated in the appearance, six million years ago, of *Pliohippus*, the predecessor of *Equus caballus*, the modern horse, 120 cm high at the withers, with improved sight and hearing and, most important, a single toe, the hoof. While these "prototypes" of the horse became extinct elsewhere, in Europe, Asia and Africa three different types of primitive horses began to develop: the Przewalski, the last wild horse that still exists in Mongolia, the Tarpan, of which there are still some individuals that were "recreated" in Poland and the Ukraine, and the Forest Horse that lived in the marshlands of northern Europe and is believed to be the ancestor of the heavy workhorse breeds of today.

It is difficult to date precisely the moment when the horse first encountered man. It appears that initially the primitive men of the Asian steppes and the European forests considered the horse as a resource: its meat for food, its coat for clothing and its bones to make tools. Subsequently, with the advent of agriculture, people began to tame horses and use them to tow wagons for transport. This also represented an important moment in the evolutionary history of man, who could thus move and travel faster.

The horse therefore became indispensable in people's daily lives and, over the following centuries, would become a determining factor in the history of humankind, becoming a major player not only in working life and transport, but also in the great migratory movements, regaining new areas in North America, from which it had virtually disappeared. Strangely enough, it is precisely in North America that the most precious fossils to

1 *The robust and powerful Friesian, with its glossy black coat, was used in the Middle Ages as a warhorse. With its imposing stature and graceful gait, it is still an excellent parade horse.*

2-3 *A Haflinger or Avelignese with its colt: small but strong and sturdy, these horses with an elegant bearing are suitable for both adults and children, thanks to their likability and their docile and gentle nature.*

4-5 *In this typical late winter Icelandic landscape, the grass is starting to sprout through the last of the snow. This is the main source of food for these horses with different coats that graze here and there in the herd, choosing the best clumps of grass.*

Many breeds and just as many stories

reconstruct the evolution of the ancestors of the modern horse have been found. At the end of the Pliocene Era, major climate changes had forced the first equids to seek refuge in South America or across the Bering Strait – which was frozen at the time – both to Asia and Europe (where, as already mentioned, they gave rise to three types of primitive horses). In North America the horse became almost extinct as a result of successive and wide spread epidemics. It was reintroduced by the Spanish conquistadors in the 16th century.

The horse was also decisive in war, especially with the advent of cavalry that in all periods of history played the leading role in the most important conquests. It is no coincidence, then, that the Arabian horse and its most direct descendant, the Spanish horse – both ancestors of all modern riding and driving horses as well as the English Thoroughbred -- are closely linked to the long domination, all over Europe, of two of the greatest conquering peoples: the Moors and the Spanish. Indeed, many examples confirm the link that has always existed between military power and the influence of certain peoples over others, for example, the Mongols and the Teutonic Knights. In addition to the expansion of Islam and of the Spanish, a third factor related to a particular group has been crucial in the spreading of the horse, not so much from a breeding point of view but from a cultural standpoint. It is the influence exercised by the great equestrian traditions of "Her Majesty's subjects," the people from Commonwealth countries, who exported their love of riding and horse racing all over the world. At the end of the 18th century in England, the Thoroughbred was born

out of this passion. Today Thoroughbreds are used to improve all the other breeds all over the world.

Thoroughbreds can claim the great merit of promoting a new field for deploying the horse: in games and sports. The newfound importance of this animal in a different field proved to be decisive for its fate. From the mid-19th century onward, with the advent of the industrial revolution and widespread mechanization, the horse lost its importance for work and as a source of power. Replaced by tractors, cars and tanks, initially the horse risked extinction in some cases. But as its role changed in the middle of the last century, it began to reinvent itself as an athlete, a sports horse and a companion for games and adventure, thereby guaranteeing its survival, which would otherwise have been uncertain. And this is how new breeds of horses, especially riding horses, came about: as the results of various crossbreeding exercises and a well-defined selection dictated by man. At the same time, this led to the consolidation and revival of historic breeds, with particular reference to their territory of origin and their vocations and aptitudes.

Many sporting and competitive disciplines today – show jumping, eventing, dressage, endurance riding, Western riding and many others – are dedicated to the horse, the same horse that is also an ideal companion for pleasure riding and trekking. One of the most significant roles of horses is in the social sphere, where they are used for rehabilitation in cases of physical or psychological disability. The role of the horse in society is extremely important and is well summed up by this historic saying: "A horse without a rider is still a horse; a rider without a horse is no longer a rider ..."

7 AN ELEGANT LUSITANO, "FRAMED" BY ONE OF THE DOORS OF AN ARENA, EXPRESSES PERFECTLY THE STRONG BOND THAT EXISTS IN PORTUGAL BETWEEN MEN, HORSES AND BULLFIGHTS, WHICH, UNLIKE THOSE IN SPAIN, DO NOT END WITH THE KILLING OF THE BULL.

10-11 THE APPALOOSA AND THE MINI APPALOOSA WERE OBTAINED THROUGH A LONG AND CAREFUL SELECTION PROCESS. THEY ARE SURE-FOOTED, AGILE AND FAST HORSES THAT CAN MANAGE ON ALL TYPES OF TERRAIN AND ALONG NARROW PATHS, GOING UPHILL OR DOWNHILL AND ALONG RIVER BANKS.

12-13 THE EYES OF THIS CONNEMARA PONY ARE LARGE, DEEP AND DARK. THE DIGNIFIED BUT GENTLE EXPRESSION REVEALS THE PRIDE AND, AT THE SAME TIME, THE DOCILITY AND INTELLIGENCE OF THIS BREED.

Five gaits for a horse

ICELAND

BECAUSE OF ITS HEIGHT, AT MOST 145 CM AT THE WITHERS, IT COULD BE CLASSIFIED AS A PONY, BUT WOE BETIDE ANYBODY WHO CALLS THE ICELANDIC HORSE A PONY IN FRONT OF AN ICELANDIC BREEDER!

The proud breeders of the Icelandic "horse" are not at all concerned about the size of their extraordinary creatures because these horses display so many desirable qualities over the diverse terrains and climatic conditions of Iceland. It is a land of fire and ice, whose conditions only a few living creatures, man included, can withstand. Even though global conventions classify the Icelandic Horse as a pony, the local people certainly consider it a horse to all intents and purposes. It has always played a central role in the lives of the local population: the particular orography of the island (the first roads that were good enough to be called roads date only from the early 1950s), allowed the Icelandic Horse to maintain its important role on farms and in families in Iceland. With the advent of cars since World War II, horses have gradually been replaced by Jeeps and off-road transport, but these animals have neither lost their identity nor has their use declined. Indeed, they are still widely used especially in the daily work with sheep, and are great companions for farmers and rural workers. Icelanders have always been dedicated to sheep farming; sheep and horses are the undisputed masters of the island's unspoiled areas.

These horses are used to living outdoors all year round and for centuries they have shared with the sheep the vast pastures that they leave only in the fall. Their sure-footedness and singular gait (the result of centuries of outdoor life), along with their powerful muscles and solid bone structure, have made them greatly appreciated in this specific context, where their qualities find full expression and are actually enhanced by the extreme environmental conditions. The Icelandic Horse is known as the "horse with five gaits" and it is famous for one of these in particular, the *tölt*, an ambling gait that is fast, smooth, sure, comfortable and suitable for even the roughest types of terrain. In addition to pace *(fetgangur)*, trot *(Brokk)* and gallop *(stokke)*, this horse is able to perform both the *tölt* and the amble *(Skeid)* naturally.

There is no vista or panorama on the island that does not feature these elegant little horses, with their coats of a vast range of colors and combinations, over 15 in all.

14 *Snow is a congenial element to the Icelandic Horse, which can move with agility in these conditions. This contributes to the development of its strong muscles.*

15 *These frugal and sturdy horses are accustomed to living outdoors all year round. In winter they are covered with long thick hair that protects them from the cold and harsh weather.*

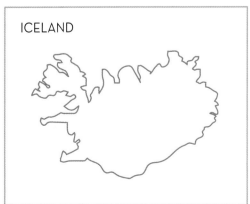

ICELAND

In winter, they grow a thicker coat that helps to protect them from bad weather. At the end of April, these horses are sent up to the mountains where, as the snow melts, the first tender shoots of grass appear. In these vast open spaces, they spend the whole summer and they reproduce. Before the winter, they go back to a location in the vicinity of their farms, where, only in extreme cases, they are fed with hay and fodder in addition to the food they procure themselves. Hardiness and efficiency are the typical characteristics of Icelandic horses; these, together with a very particular nature, make them truly unique horses. Without any effort, they can carry a weight equal to one-third of their own

(unlike most other breeds, in which this ratio is one-fifth) and can tow one and a half times their own weight. Their muscle power allows them to endure someone in the saddle for hours, both during hard days' work with the flocks and also for leisure activities, for example, on long, challenging trekking trips. Being so athletic, they have great success in sports: indeed, they are used in the spectacular *tölt* events; competitions dedicated to this extraordinary gait.

16 *Two young colts challenge each other playfully. This activity is very important for all animals that live in herds; it reinforces their ties and strengthens their character.*

16-17 *There is no corner of Iceland without these horses living in the wild. In late April, when the snow melts, they are sent to graze up on the mountains where the first tender shoots of grass sprout.*

18-19 *The qualities of this little horse enable it to survive in the difficult Icelandic climate. Its sure-footedness and solid bone structure make it a truly exceptional animal.*

20 *In mountainous areas in summer, the grass is thick and lush and newborn foals grow strong and healthy, ready to become the exceptional companions of people working in the area.*

21 *Their strong and stocky structure, with sturdy well-proportioned limbs, allows these horses to carry a weight equal to one-third of their own, while as draft horses they can tow a weight equal to one-and-a-half times their own.*

22 *Icelandic horses still live in the wild, feeding on what the territory offers them. Being a very important workforce for the population, they are safeguarded and protected.*

22-23 *The Icelandic is best known for the distinction of having five gaits. In addition to the walk, trot and canter, the Icelandic can amble and perform the tölt, which is a sort of fast walk.*

The horses of the Valkyries

NORWAY

IN NORSE MYTHOLOGY,
THE FJORD HORSE WAS
THE STEED OF THE VALKYRIES.
TODAY IT IS A VERSATILE
AND RELIABLE PONY.

Horses seem to have the ability to fire up the imagination and bring to mind myths, legends and images out of dreams. Ancient Norse mythology associated with the world of the Vikings tells of horses with golden coats, small in stature but of exceptional strength, ridden by the Valkyries and beloved by the gods: they were the Fjord Horses, the horses of the Norwegian fjords. Legends aside, this breed is considered one of the oldest and purest in the world. It is assumed that the ancestors of the present horses arrived in Scandinavia from Asia and that they were domesticated there about 4,000 years ago. The hostile Norwegian environment, characterized by rough rocky terrain, forged these strong and powerful animals, accentuating their hardiness and adaptability. These qualities, along with a bright but gentle temperament that facilitates training, made them excellent work and war horses for the Vikings, who took them with them whenever they set off on their daring exploits, and who started to breed them. They were one of the very first peoples to use the horse in agriculture, attaching it to the plow. In addition to working in the fields, Fjord Horses were soon both saddled and harnessed, and used as packhorses. Because of their versatility, they have always been the extraordinary companions of breeders and farmers, and indeed, in some remote and inaccessible areas in Norway even today, Fjord Horses are considered important members of the family, and they replace machines whenever necessary.

One of the most obvious distinguishing marks of the breed is the coat. Of a uniform dun color (beige), it has a darker dorsal stripe, and sometimes zebra markings on its legs. Its coarse upright mane and its tail both have black and

24-25 *The intense bitter cold of the long Norwegian winter causes the Fjord to grow a long thick coat that protects it from the harsh conditions.*

25 *The horse, or rather, given its small stature, the pony of the Norwegian fjords, is considered to be one of the oldest and purest equine breeds in the world; it reached Scandinavia from Asia about 4,000 years ago.*

NORWAY

light, almost silver hair. Traditionally, the mane is clipped in a distinctive crescent shape, starting from the poll to the withers, following the curvature of the neck. This style of cutting means that the black hairs in the center stand above the shorter silver hairs on the outside, creating an attractive chromatic effect.

The height of the Fjord Horse can vary between 134 and 144 cm (13.2-14.2 hands) at the withers. It is therefore a pony to all intents and purposes, even though it is considered to be a horse in its homeland. Ranging from 900 to 1,200 pounds, its weight gives a good idea of its rather stocky constitution. Nonetheless, it is a good-looking horse, with balanced and rhythmic gaits.

It has the typical large head of ponies and its forehead is wide and flat, with small mobile ears. A Norwegian saying states: "Its eyes are like mountain lakes on a midsummer evening, big and bright." The neck is well-proportioned, muscular and arched. It is a muscular horse with powerful sturdy limbs, short large shins, and wide hard hooves.

And finally, its temperament, again according to a Norwegian breeders' saying, is "as lively as a waterfall in spring." Brilliant but docile, the Fjord horse is an all-rounder. In addition to work in the fields, today the Fjord Horse is successfully used for equitation, both as a pony in riding schools and for sports (jumping, dressage, endurance, harness-racing and standardbred racing). Thanks to its considerable psycho-physical balance, it is also used for hippotherapy.

26-27 IT HAS A SPECIAL COAT OF A DUN COLOR THAT IS MARKED BY A DARK DORSAL STRIPE. ITS THICK COARSE MANE AND ITS TAIL BOTH HAVE BLACK AND LIGHT, ALMOST SILVER HAIR.

27 IT WAS THE VIKINGS, ONE OF THE FIRST PEOPLE TO USE THE HORSE IN AGRICULTURE, WHO STARTED TO BREED FJORDS, WHICH, IN SOME AREAS, STILL REPLACE MACHINES.

28-29 TRADITIONALLY, THE MANE IS CLIPPED IN A DISTINCTIVE CRESCENT SHAPE FROM THE POLL TO THE WITHERS, FOLLOWING THE CURVATURE OF THE NECK. THIS GIVES THE FJORD A UNIQUE APPEARANCE.

29 THE FJORD HAS A MASSIVE HEAD WITH POWERFUL JAWS, A CHARACTERISTIC THAT IS TYPICAL OF PONIES. ITS LARGE BRIGHT EYES HAVE A GENTLE EXPRESSION THAT REFLECTS ITS GOOD DISPOSITION AND DOCILE NATURE, WHICH MAKE IT SUITABLE FOR ALL USES.

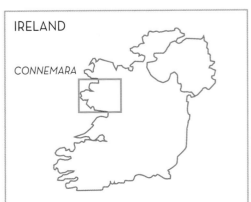

IRELAND

CONNEMARA

From the land of Eire

IRELAND ▪ CONNEMARA

SMALL BUT STRONG AND
POWERFUL, CONNEMARA PONIES
ARE EXCELLENT ATHLETES
IN EQUESTRIAN SPORTS.

County Galway in Ireland occupies a large sweep of the picturesque Atlantic coast and extends inland over a vast plain where Lough Corrib, one of the largest lakes in Ireland, lies. To the northwest lies the region of Connemara with its unusual appearance, its rugged mountains in stark contrast with the large bleak expanses of reddish peat dotted with a myriad of intense blue lakes and the Atlantic coast with its wealth of fjords and unspoiled beaches. A concentration of beauty that is so wild and unique that it deserves, at least once in a lifetime, a visit that will not be easily forgotten. The ancient Gaelic language is spoken here and the people are very friendly. This wild land is the home of the Connemara Pony that takes its name from this region.

The Connemara Pony is the product of its land. Its shape reveals the intimate relationship that exists between the environment and the development of these horses in the territory. The grass that is very nutritious and rich in minerals constitutes the basis of the horses' nutrition. Due to the influence of the Gulf Stream in this area, the grass flourishes for most of the year. The soil is rich in phosphates and other precious minerals that help to strengthen the horses. Some horses also eat the seaweed that is rich in nutrients. The vegetation is responsible for the size of ponies; indeed, there are considerable differences in height due to different places of origin that may be either more or less rich in vegetation. The Connemara Pony is successfully used in equestrian sports, and because of its size it can be mounted by both children and adults of average weight. Indeed, were it not for his height – 135 to 147 cm (13.3 to 14.5 hands) at the withers –, with its strong solid structure it could easily be taken for a horse. It is particularly appreciated for pleasure rides in the countryside and for use in harness. Moreover, Irish breeders often use Connemara mares to breed horses for equestrian competitions or to mate with English thoroughbred stallions.

30-31 *The Connemara Pony is a product of its homeland, Ireland. More precisely, it comes from the wild northwestern region overlooking the Atlantic called Connemara, whence the pony gets its name.*

30 *Lively and agile, yet strong and sturdy, Connemara Ponies are first-class athletes and they excel in various disciplines of equestrian sports.*

32-33 *The Connemara's physical constitution is more like that of a horse than a pony. This feature, combined with a height at the withers ranging from 135 to 147 cm, makes it very suitable for riding by both adults and children.*

34 *Coming from a wild land, the Connemara Pony has been strengthened so that it is naturally sturdy and brave, characteristics that it has maintained over time.*

35 *Thanks to their specific traits, Connemara Ponies are very popular for pleasure riding and trekking. Irish breeders also use Connemara mares to breed horses for equestrian competitions by crossing them with English Thoroughbred stallions.*

The Precious Piebald

IRELAND

"GYPSY GOLD DOES NOT CHINK AND GLITTER.
IT GLEAMS IN THE SUN AND NEIGHS IN THE DARK."

Gypsies are nomadic people par excellence and, through the centuries, the horse has always been necessary for their travels. What binds these people to horses, however, is not only dependence but above all love and respect. So much so that the Gypsies of the British Isles created a breed of strong, tireless, versatile, gentle and faithful horses that are also popular among those who do not belong to this ethnic group: the Irish Cob.

The morphological development of these horses is indeed due to the passion of the gypsies of England and Ireland who started breeding these extraordinary horses. What make them particularly fascinating are their strong, sturdy structure, their extremely beautiful piebald coat, abundant tail and mane, and the feathering that completely covers the hooves and rises up almost to the knees. It is said that the ones with dappled coats were very much desired because, being easily recognizable, they were more difficult to steal.

The Irish Cob is known by different names, the most famous being Gypsy Vanner, by which it is known, in particular, in America. Another name is Tinker Horse, as many a Gypsy practiced the ambulant tinsmith trade with the aid of his horse. Other names are Gypsy Cob, Traditional Cob, Colored Cob, Backy and Blattie ... all these names have caused confusion, giving the impression that they were different breeds. In reality, there is only one breed, called by different names depending on the country because Gypsies, being nomads, are considered a people without a country and consequently, nothing that belongs to them, including horses, has a geographical location or a precise definition.

Moreover, Gypsy culture is traditionally handed down by word of mouth and is not written down. For this reason, there is no documented history of this horse.

36 THE IRISH COB ALSO HAS OTHER NAMES, THE MOST FAMOUS BEING GYPSY VANNER, THE NAME BY WHICH IT IS KNOWN, IN PARTICULAR, IN AMERICA.

37 THE GYPSY VANNER COMES FROM THE BRITISH ISLES. INDEED, IT WAS THE LOCAL GYPSIES WHO TURNED IT INTO A STRONG AND TIRELESS BREED TO SUIT THEIR NEEDS.

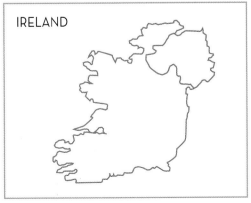

IRELAND

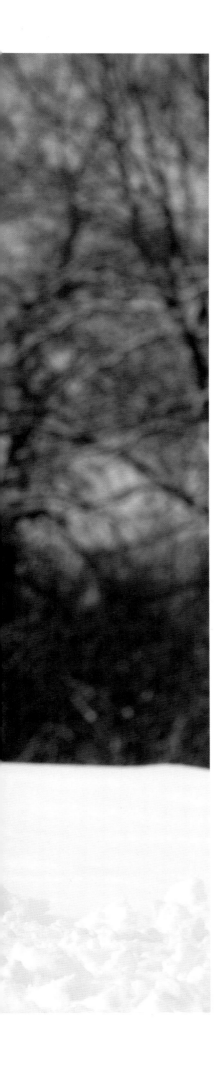

38-39 *Features that make these horses particularly fascinating are their rugged, beautiful piebald coats, their thick tails and manes and the feathering that covers their hooves.*

39 TOP *It is said that the piebald coat was a much desired, purpose-developed feature. Being easily recognizable, a horse with a piebald coat was rarely stolen as it could be easily identified.*

39 BOTTOM *Their strength, resistance to different climates, versatility and docility made these horses ideal for the Gypsies' long wagon journeys.*

It is believed that it is the result of crossbreeding between Shire, Clydesdale, Friesian and Dales Pony, Fell and Galloway breeds. It was born and bred as a light draft horse, suitable for the brightly colored caravans in which the gypsies lived and moved about, and has subsequently proved to be an excellent riding horse.

Today, the Irish Cob is still considered a symbol of wealth among Gypsies. Many Gypsies are currently selling their horses to non-Gypsies. Indeed, the Irish Cob's courage and strength make it perfect for the country and for cross-country events. It is also endowed with elegant gaits

and good jumping agility. Being patient and of a pleasant disposition, it is suitable for all riders, including children.

The Irish Cob is no longer used for transport by Gypsies in their itinerant life. If you cross the Irish countryside, however, is not difficult to come across colorful caravans pulled by these horses. You will find, however, that the caravans contain not Gypsies, but tourists on vacation. A trip in a caravan pulled by a splendid Irish Cob is, indeed, one of the classic holidays proposed by the Tourist Board of Ireland.

40 *THE MORPHOLOGICAL FEATURES OF THE GYPSY VANNER ARE EVIDENT EVEN IN FOALS. ITS LIMBS ARE STRONG AND STURDY, ITS BODY IS COMPACT AND SOLID AND ITS GAITS ARE WIDE AND GRACEFUL.*

40-41 *THE MARKINGS VARY IN COLOR AND SHAPE. IRISH COBS, BORN AND BRED FOR LIGHT DRAFT WORK, HAVE ALSO PROVED TO BE PARTICULARLY GOOD RIDING HORSES, ESPECIALLY FOR PLEASURE RIDING IN THE COUNTRY.*

42-43 Irish Cobs are no longer used by Gypsies in their itinerant lifestyle. Crossing the countryside, however, is not unusual to see them pulling colorful caravans of tourists.

UNITED KINGDOM

SHETLAND ISLANDS

The smallest in the world

UNITED KINGDOM ■ SHETLAND ISLANDS

WITH ITS PLUMP BODY AND SHORT LEGS IT LOOKS RATHER
FUNNY AND PARTICULARLY ENDEARING ... BUT BEWARE,
THE SHETLAND PONY IS VERY PROUD AND INDEPENDENT.

Although it is the world's smallest, the Shetland pony deserves respect because of the important role it plays in the equestrian world. Thanks to its docile nature, its intelligence and adaptability, and also thanks to being of just the right height, the Shetland pony is well-suited to shoulder a very important responsibility: to be the perfect friend and companion of children in their first encounters with horse riding.

Although there are different theories about their origins, we can safely say that the Shetland Islands in northeastern Scotland are the homeland of these small, funny but very intelligent ponies. Indeed, thanks to its docile nature, combined with a very attentive and alert spirit and being extremely sensitivity, the Shetland pony is not only the king of pony schools for children but is also widely used in hippotherapy for children with physical and mental disabilities.

Frugal and sturdy, this pony has survived very difficult environmental conditions that have forged its physical characteristics as well as its temperament. In the Shetland Islands, there is nowhere that is further than 5 km from the sea. Whenever food was very scarce, the ponies would go down to the sea side to feed on seaweed. Only the strongest survived the harsh winters and so natural selection caused the breed to become stronger and sturdier over time. The sturdiness of the Shetland pony is legendary, to the extent that it is considered to be the strongest of all horse breeds. Indeed, the Shetland pony is the only pony that can tow a load that is twice its weight, a feat that is impossible for any other pony.

According to the official English register, the maximum permitted height of a Shetland pony is 106.7 cm (10.5 hands) at the withers. Its coat can be of various colors and its mane and tail should be very thick and abundant; its tail should almost touch the ground and its forelock should reach its muzzle. Dedicated and extremely courageous, the Shetland pony is a tireless worker and its adaptability enables it to learn everything quickly and to carry out its tasks with patience and diligence. The Shetland pony's main use today is in pleasure riding and teaching for children, or in pulling small elegant gigs. Thanks to their longevity – they can live for more than 30 years – Shetland ponies can be companions for life. Shetland Ponies are bred mainly in England, where thousands of them are born each year, but they are common all over the world.

44-45 AS A FOAL, THE SHETLAND PONY LOOKS LIKE A PUPPY THAT AROUSES ENDEARMENT AND
AFFECTION. EVEN WHEN THEY ARE STILL SMALL, THESE PONIES HAVE A THICK FUR, AN ABUNDANT
FORELOCK, SMALL EARS AND THE FUNNY MANNERISMS THAT ARE TYPICAL OF THE BREED.

44 TWO COLTS PLAY WITH EACH OTHER ON FOULA IN THE SHETLAND ISLANDS, THE HOMELAND
OF THIS CHARMING, YET STRONG AND STURDY PONY. THE SMALL ISLAND HAS FEW INHABITANTS,
BUT ON THE OTHER HAND, IT IS HOME TO MANY OF THESE LITTLE EQUINES.

46-47 *THE STRONG WILD NATURE OF THESE LANDS WITH SUCH WONDERFUL LANDSCAPES HAS FORGED THE CONSTITUTION AND CHARACTER OF THE SHETLAND PONY. THE LATTER IS MUCH MORE DOCILE AND GENTLE THAN THIS CURIOUS PICTURE WOULD SUGGEST.*

48 AS WITH HORSES, THE MORPHOLOGY OF PONIES CHANGES SIGNIFICANTLY DEPENDING ON THEIR HABITAT. THE PHYSICAL CHARACTERISTICS OF THE SHETLAND PONY ALLOW IT TO LIVE IN VERY HARSH CLIMATIC AND NUTRITIONAL CONDITIONS.

49 THE MINI SHETLAND PONY, LIKE ALL OTHER MINI PONIES, IS NOT THE PRODUCT OF NATURE BUT OF A LONG AND CAREFUL SELECTION BY MAN TO GENERATE SMALL HORSES AS PETS FOR CHILDREN.

The gentle giant

UNITED KINGDOM

THE SHIRE HORSE IS THE LARGEST IN THE WORLD.

The British Isles boast many fine horses and ponies. But the Shire horse is the most famous for both its quality and its massive size, which makes it the biggest horse in the world. The ancestor of the Shire horse, known by its Latin name *magnus equus*, was much appreciated for its size and strength even at the time of the Roman conquest of Britain. The first written records of the huge horse date back to the 12th century. There is a written account, dated 1154, of a fair held in Smithfield with these great horses. Subsequently, this breed of giants, which had been used only as cart horses or working horses, began to appear in battle and in chivalrous tournaments. According to numerous sources, draft stallions from Flanders and Holland were imported to improve its stock. Indeed, royal edicts of the Kings of England encouraged the breeding of horses of increasing size and muscular mass to withstand the heavy trappings of horse and rider.

In the Middle Ages, these large horses were known by various names that recalled their qualities and characteristics - Great Horse, Strong Horse, Warhorse, Old English Black Horse - while the common use of the name Shire Horse goes back to the statutes of Henry VIII. When the days of armor and tournaments were over, the ancient horse was again used as a working horse or a cart horse, until 1877, when the Shire Horse Society, an association of British breeders, was founded. The Breed Stud Book was created in 1879 and the first show at the Royal Agricultural Hall in Islington was held in 1886 on the initiative of King George V.

Since 1961, the Shire Horse Society Spring Show has been held at the end of March in Peterborough, where the society has its headquarters. It is one of the most spectacular equestrian events, with visitors coming from all over the world. While sheer size and strength have been its fundamental features, the Shire Horse is now recognized for its distinction and its lively gaits. Despite their size, once in motion, Shire Horses are lively, graceful and elegant. Considering that these animals can be up to 180 cm (17.7 hands) tall at the withers and weigh more than a ton, their class and agility are all the more evident. Other distinguishing features of these modern giants are the tufts of hair called feathers around their legs, which start at the hooves and often go all the way up their shanks. These hairy coverings protect the horse's legs from the damp in farmland and today they are particularly well-groomed as they are elements of assessment in horse shows. The Shire Horse, however, remains a perfect towing machine, a horse that can easily transport up to three or four times its own weight without too much effort. Indeed, this is the typical image that comes from the Anglo-Saxon world, a Shire Horse pulling a wagon of beer kegs. Intelligent and easy to train, thanks to the fact that they are so calm and good natured, Shire Horses are portrayed not only pulling carts but also saddled or on a long reins. There is probably no horse show in the world that has not hosted, at least once, one of these giants of the world of horses.

50-51 *Although they may exceed 180 cm in height at the withers and may weigh more than a ton, Shires move with agility, smooth gaits and unexpected grace.*

50 *The Shire horse is the largest in the world and among the most easily identified, thanks to the typical feathering on its legs. These are just two of the features that make it famous and popular throughout the world.*

52 *Today the Shire has returned to its origins and is used for transport. In the Middle Ages, however, it was also used in battle and in tournaments, thus proving that it had remarkable qualities as a riding horse.*

52-53 *Because of its size, the ancestor of the Shire was known by the Latin name of magnus equus, meaning "big horse." Its descendant displays all the might and strength that the name suggests as it can tow wagons, carriages and agricultural equipment with ease.*

UNITED
KINGDOM

ASCOT

A royal racecourse

UNITED KINGDOM ■ ASCOT

FOUNDED BY A QUEEN OF ENGLAND, ASCOT IS ONE
OF THE TEMPLES OF HORSE RACING AND BRITISH HIGH SOCIETY.

It was in the early summer of 1711 that Queen Anne of England, a great lover of hunting and horse racing, was riding in a horse-drawn carriage when she came across an area of open heath in what is now called Ascot (then called East Cote), recently acquired by the Crown, not far from Windsor Castle. She felt that it was an ideal place for "horses to gallop at full stretch." This is how the Queen decided to build a race track there.

Work began quickly and on 11 August of that year, in Her Majesty's presence, Ascot hosted its first race, called "Her Majesty's Plate," worth 100 guineas and open to any stallion or mare. This is how one of the temples of thoroughbred racing was born. It is a place where even today, despite the modern infrastructure that has been added to the racecourse over the years, you can breathe three centuries of history. In truth, Ascot is one of the few sporting venues that have such an illustrious tradition. The mere fact that the elliptical path of the track, on which the strongest English thoroughbreds in the world compete, has remained unchanged for 300 years makes it an almost magical place.

Kings and queens of England have always attended the races, arriving at the racetrack from nearby Windsor Castle. Their arrival in the royal carriage makes the event even more solemn, one of the most sought-after social engagements of the nobility. To this day Ascot remains a true national institution for England. Indeed, Royal Ascot is one of the most important events of the British social calendar, at which it is more important to be seen than to see. A must for nobles, the bourgeoisie and members of high society, who aim to secure a place in the Royal Enclosure, a large area with all the amenities reserved for the Queen and her guests. The dress code for men is rigid, black or gray morning dress and top hat, while the ladies are allowed to show off refined "apparel" enriched by colorful hats. Ascot has always been synonymous with elegance, a perfect synthesis of tradition, style and fashion.

During the year, Ascot stages 25 days of racing, of which 16 occur between May and October. The highlight of the Royal Meeting, held in June, is the Gold Cup, which is run over 2 miles and 4 furlongs, followed in importance by the Queen Anne Stakes, which is run over 1 mile in honor of Ascot's founder. The most prestigious race, however, is the King George VI and Queen Elizabeth Stakes in July, a race reserved for English Thoroughbreds 3 years and older. Run over a distance of 1 mile and 4 furlongs, it has a purse of 1 million pounds. Only two horses, Dahlia (1973 and 1974) and Swain (1997 and 1998), have managed to win this race twice, but many champions of all time, including the great Ribot, appear on the competition's roll of honor.

54-55 *ALTHOUGH 300 YEARS HAVE PASSED SINCE ITS INAUGURATION, ASCOT IS STILL A UNIQUE PLACE. ITS CHARM REMAINS UNCHANGED NOTWITHSTANDING THE MANY MODERN EXTENSIONS.*

54 *THE RACETRACK IS THE SYMBOL AND THE HEART OF ASCOT. THE MOST FAMOUS ENGLISH THOROUGHBREDS IN THE HISTORY OF HORSE RACING HAVE ALL RUN AT ASCOT WHERE THE RACETRACK LAYOUT HAS REMAINED PRACTICALLY UNCHANGED SINCE ITS INCEPTION.*

56 AUGUST 11TH, 1711 IS A MEMORABLE DATE FOR ASCOT AND THE HISTORY OF HORSE RACING. IT IS THE DATE OF THE FIRST EDITION OF THE FAMOUS RACE, "HER MAJESTY'S PLATE." THE PRIZE MONEY FOR THE WINNER WAS 100 GUINEAS

56-57 ASCOT BELONGS TO THE CROWN ESTATE OF THE UNITED KINGDOM AND IT IS VERY MUCH A NATIONAL INSTITUTION. THE NUMBER OF SPECTATORS HAS RECENTLY EXCEEDED THE HALF A MILLION MARK IN A YEAR.

58 *The racing calendar at Ascot is full of top-class meetings. The Royal Meeting that is held in June has a worldwide following as it is the most prestigious horse race meeting in Europe.*

59 *Many important races are held at Ascot. The King George VI and Queen Elizabeth Stakes in July is an opportunity that can boost the career of an English four year old Thoroughbred to stardom.*

60-61 *To win at Ascot is to earn a place in the horse racing hall of fame. It is not quite within the reach of most horses, and indeed there have only been two horses to win the King George VI and Queen Elizabeth Stakes more than once.*

UNITED
KINGDOM

LONDON

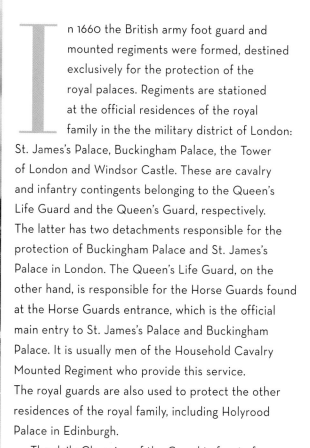

The Queen's Guard

UNITED KINGDOM ▪ LONDON

THE BRITISH MONARCHY MAINTAINS ONE OF
THE MOST EXTRAORDINARY TRADITIONS, THAT
OF THE HORSE GUARDS WHO GO ON PARADE
EVERY DAY DURING THE CHANGING OF THE GUARD
CEREMONY AT BUCKINGHAM PALACE.

In 1660 the British army foot guard and mounted regiments were formed, destined exclusively for the protection of the royal palaces. Regiments are stationed at the official residences of the royal family in the the military district of London: St. James's Palace, Buckingham Palace, the Tower of London and Windsor Castle. These are cavalry and infantry contingents belonging to the Queen's Life Guard and the Queen's Guard, respectively. The latter has two detachments responsible for the protection of Buckingham Palace and St. James's Palace in London. The Queen's Life Guard, on the other hand, is responsible for the Horse Guards found at the Horse Guards entrance, which is the official main entry to St. James's Palace and Buckingham Palace. It is usually men of the Household Cavalry Mounted Regiment who provide this service. The royal guards are also used to protect the other residences of the royal family, including Holyrood Palace in Edinburgh.

The daily Changing of the Guard in front of Buckingham Palace takes place at 11:30 a.m. and lasts 30 minutes. It is held every day from May to July and every other day in autumn and winter, but may be canceled in the event of rain. To protect the royal palace during the Changing of the Guard, a detachment of Horse Guards leaves the Hyde Park barracks to go to that of the Horse Guards, passing in front of Buckingham Palace to coincide with the Guard Mounting. The Changing of the Guard takes place in front of this renowned royal residence and is one of the most famous ceremonies in the world. The same solemn changeover can also be seen at Windsor Castle.

The Guards' horses are generally black or dark bay. They are all of good stature, strong and powerful, and structurally very similar to each other so as to create a harmonious effect on parade. Well-behaved, well-trained and patient, they come forward neatly lined up in rows. All the horses of the Queen's Guard are kept in stables adjoining Buckingham Palace, enlarged by architect John Nash (1752-1835), who designed the reconstruction of the entire building.

62-63 *THE DAILY CHANGING OF THE GUARD AT BUCKINGHAM PALACE IS ONE OF THE MOST FAMOUS TRADITIONS OF THE ENGLISH MONARCHY AND ONE OF THE UNMISSABLE EVENTS DURING A VISIT TO LONDON.*

62 *THE CEREMONY TAKES PLACE AT 11:30 A.M. AND LASTS 30 MINUTES, BUT THE FIRST GUARDS ARRIVE 15 MINUTES EARLIER TOGETHER WITH A MILITARY BAND. IT'S 45 MINUTES OF PURE EMOTION.*

64-65 *While the guard is being changed, the palace is left unguarded. For this reason, a detachment of Horse Guards passes in front of Buckingham Palace at that precise moment to ensure its defense.*

66 *The training of the horses is very important, because they must be able to stand still for a long time and to come forward neatly lined up in rows, at the same pace.*

66-67 *The horses do not belong to any specific breed. They are generally very dark bay or black horses and they are housed in the stables of Buckingham Palace.*

68-69 THE FRIESIAN HORSE IS NATIVE TO THE FAMOUS ISLANDS LOCATED A FEW
KILOMETERS OFF THE DUTCH, GERMAN AND DANISH COASTS IN THE NORTH SEA,
WITHIN EASY REACH OF THE COAST AT LOW TIDE, ON FOOT OR ON HORSEBACK.

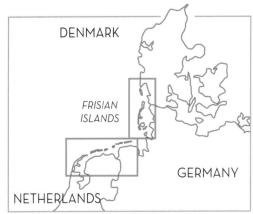

DENMARK

FRISIAN
ISLANDS

GERMANY

NETHERLANDS

Straight from the middle ages

DENMARK, GERMANY, NETHERLANDS ▪ FRISIAN ISLANDS

THE GLOSSY COAT OF THE FRIESIAN HORSE
HAS WITNESSED CENTURIES OF HISTORY.

If there is a horse that is capable of bridging the gap between centuries, it is the Friesian. Even today, it is still capable of taking man back to a time when this steed, with a pitch black coat, was the favorite mount of generals and warlords. Indeed, because of the way it has its evolved, the Friesian represents a historical period. It is a horse that has come to us straight from the Middle Ages. It is no coincidence, then, that the strong link between the Friesian and this period of history (and the iconography connected to it) has made it the undisputed favorite for jousting contests and historical costume re-enactments, for circus acts, high school shows, and film productions. Its morphology and distinguishing characteristics have remained largely unchanged after many centuries of history.

The Frisian Islands, the birthplace of the breed, form an archipelago that extends, only a few kilometers off the coastline, from Holland to Germany and Denmark. The islands are well-known for their unusual orographic characteristics: at low tide they can be reached from the coast on foot or horseback, following muddy narrow strips of land that emerge as the tide goes out. The Friesian developed in this area with its special ecoclimate, and subsequently became a well-known and appreciated horse that is bred in many parts of the world. It has always been considered a multi-purpose horse due to its sturdy build, its agility and intelligence and its pleasant disposition toward man.

The Friesian has proved, through the ages, that it is very suitable for riding and, above all, for deployment in farm work and as a draft horse. For centuries, these exceptional horses have been the faithful companions of the inhabitants of Friesland and of neighboring Germany, assisting them in all their daily activities, in times of peace and in times of war. These black Nordic horses even followed the Teutonic knights to the Crusades, and it was probably in the Holy Land that they first came into contact with the fiery little horses of the desert. With the injection of Arab blood, which made the Friesians even better as "steeds," or shall we say riding horses, they became extremely widespread and popular, as indeed one can infer from the many paintings by 15th century artists of the Flemish school that depict them. They became the preferred mounts of nobles, knights and warlords because of their ability to bear the weight of the riders and their heavy armor and, at the same time, display great agility and speed, indispensable qualities to withstand attacks in battles and duels.

During the Spanish occupation of Holland, between the 16th and 17th centuries, the Friesian was crossed with fine Andalusian and Oriental horses that passed on their brisk high-stepping trot, making the breed very suitable for carriage driving. This new type, in addition to being a warhorse, endorsed its success as an "improver" breed, which allowed the Friesian, through the export of prize specimens, to contribute – directly and indirectly – with its genes to many other breeds of Standardbred horses. What is striking about this massive horse is its imposing stature and the characteristic feathering around its hooves. But the Friesian is at its best when in movement. Thanks to its energy and its spectacular high-stepping trot, it becomes almost graceful, and the undulating of its thick flowing mane and tail almost creates the illusion that it is dancing. Today, Friesians are bred more or less all over the world, and there are many associations that are recognized by the Friesch Paarden Stamboek of Drachten in the Netherlands, the association that keeps the Stud Book of the breed.

70 *A MULTIPURPOSE ANIMAL, THANKS TO ITS VIGOR, AGILITY, INTELLIGENCE AND BEING SO WELL DISPOSED TOWARD MAN, THE FRIESIAN HORSE IS FOUND IN MANY COUNTRIES. AN AGILE DRAFT HORSE, THE FRIESIAN HAS BECOME A BREED THAT IS USED TO "IMPROVE" OTHERS.*

71 *THE SPANISH OCCUPATION OF THE NETHERLANDS IN THE 16TH AND 17TH CENTURIES, ALONG WITH THE INEVITABLE CROSSING OF LOCAL HORSES WITH THE ELEGANT IBERIAN HORSES, LED TO THE FURTHER DEVELOPMENT OF THE FRIESIAN BREED.*

72-73 *IN ACTION, THE FRIESIAN IS TRANSFORMED, SHOWING VIGOROUS BUT ELASTIC GAITS AND MOVEMENTS. THE SWAY OF THE THICK MANE MAKES ITS MOVEMENTS EVEN MORE GRACEFUL, ALMOST LIKE A DANCE, AND ITS BLACK, GLOSSY COAT ACCENTUATES ITS ELEGANCE.*

GERMANY

ROTTACH-EGERN

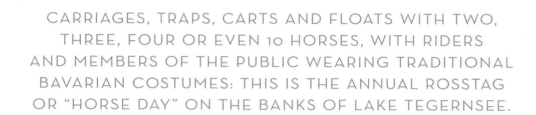

Horse Day

GERMANY ▪ ROTTACH-EGERN

CARRIAGES, TRAPS, CARTS AND FLOATS WITH TWO, THREE, FOUR OR EVEN 10 HORSES, WITH RIDERS AND MEMBERS OF THE PUBLIC WEARING TRADITIONAL BAVARIAN COSTUMES: THIS IS THE ANNUAL ROSSTAG OR "HORSE DAY" ON THE BANKS OF LAKE TEGERNSEE.

In Bavaria in southeastern Germany, on the border with Austria. Deeper into the territory, the scenery becomes greener, the vegetation is richer and more lush and colorful, and the air is cool and crisp. Rottach-Egern is a resort in the valley of the Tegernsee, one of the cleanest lakes in the world. The turquoise water is crystal clear and it is so pure that you can drink it. Every year on the last Sunday of August, at the end of the summer season, Rottach-Egern is the scene of the Rosstag, the traditional folk festival dedicated to horses.

And every year, this important event attracts traditional carts from Bavaria, Tyrol, Austria and all the surrounding areas to this beautiful tourist resort. A festival in which the protagonist is the horse, against the fantastic scenery that extends from the shores of the lake to the heart of the surrounding countryside. The place is teeming with horses of many different breeds that are all carefully and elegantly groomed. Haflingers, Westfalens, Oldenburgers, Holsteiners, Friesians, Lipizzaners, Appaloosas, Welsh Ponies, Shetland Ponies, Connemaras and mules ... all sorts of horses, big and small, and with every type of coat. The male and female riders are all dressed in traditional Bavarian costumes, keeping up a custom of great historical

importance. The carts are original, brightly colored and decorated with flowers. The long parade leaves at 10:30 a.m. from the Seehotel Überfahrt on the shores of the lake, accompanied by a Bavarian band, and it winds as far as the eye can see along the entire perimeter of the lake, to a point where the road turns into the surrounding countryside to reach a wide clearing where all the participants parade in front of a huge crowd of spectators who join in the procession. And it is all surrounded by wooden tables with an abundance of pitchers of beer and sandwiches for all. One big festival that is well worth attending, a holiday marked by the presence of horses in a land of ancient folk traditions.

74-75 *EVERY YEAR ON THE LAST SUNDAY OF AUGUST, THE TOWN OF ROTTACH-EGERN IN BAVARIA HOSTS ONE OF THE MOST TRADITIONAL FOLK FESTIVALS OF THE EQUESTRIAN WORLD, THE ROSSTAG.*

74 *THE HORSES BELONG TO A WIDE VARIETY OF BREEDS. ELEGANTLY GROOMED WITH GREAT CARE AND ADORNED WITH BRIGHT AND COLORFUL TRAPPINGS AND DECORATIONS, THEY ARE ACCOMPANIED BY PEOPLE WEARING TRADITIONAL BAVARIAN COSTUMES.*

75 *THE ROSSTAG HAS A VERY OLD TRADITION THAT ATTRACTS, IN ADDITION TO THE PEOPLE OF BAVARIA, TYROLEAN AND AUSTRIAN NEIGHBORS WHO TRAVEL TO THE AREA WITH THEIR CARTS PULLED BY DRAFT HORSES OF THE NATIVE BREEDS, SUCH AS THIS BEAUTIFUL PAIR.*

76 EVEN AT OTHER TIMES OF THE YEAR, ROTTACH-EGERN STAGES IMPORTANT EQUESTRIAN EVENTS AND SHOWS, FEATURING MANY DIFFERENT BREEDS OF HORSES FROM VARIOUS PLACES OF ORIGIN.

76-77 TRADITIONAL SLEIGHS PULLED BY THE FAST AGILE HAFLINGERS COMPETE ON THE VAST SNOW-COVERED PLAINS OF THE AREA.

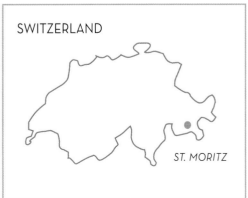

SWITZERLAND

ST. MORITZ

White Turf and Snow Polo

SWITZERLAND ■ ST. MORITZ

A SERIES OF EQUESTRIAN EVENTS KEEPS THE PUBLIC ENTERTAINED IN ONE OF THE MOST FAMOUS TOURIST RESORTS IN THE WORLD.

St. Moritz, in the heart of the Swiss Alps, is the country's most popular resort for winter sports. It is an elegant and much sought-after tourist resort that every year attracts a large number of skiers and mountain lovers from around the world, and it holds in store an interesting diversion for horse lovers. Every winter in January and February, this charming town offers a full program of equestrian events. On the first three Sundays of February, St. Moritz sets the scene for the White Turf meeting, which includes the traditional trotting and gallop races. The scenery is breathtaking: a 2,700-meter race track of packed snow, made with artificial snow sprayed for the occasion on the fascinating frozen lake. The horses, English thoroughbreds and trotters, challenge each other at very high speeds in a fairy-tale atmosphere. The thoroughbreds in the race can reach speeds up to 50 kmh. Apart from these exciting races, the meeting then features the exhilarating Skikjöring race where skilled skiers, often ski instructors, are towed along by galloping thoroughbreds at top speed.

78-79 *Every year the White Turf Meeting, with its traditional and exciting harness and gallop races on the snow, takes over the city of St. Moritz on the first three Sundays in February.*

78 *The racetrack is 2,700 meters long and covered with sprayed and packed artificial snow. In the background is the picturesque frozen lake.*

80 TOP *The harness races are among the most famous in their class. A stunning scenario surrounding the event attracts a wide and heterogeneous audience.*

80 BOTTOM *The races are held in the famous Swiss resort, which is a preferred destination for thousands of skiers, and which, on the occasion of the White Turf Meeting, stages a number of complementary prestige events.*

80-81 *One of the specialty events of the White Turf meeting is the exhilarating Skikjöring race where a skier is towed along by galloping Thoroughbreds at top speed.*

The meeting is a most entertaining event for lovers
of equestrian sports, but it is just as entertaining for all
the other tourists, thanks to the presence of bands on
the track, the exhibition of works of art by local artists
and the abundance of rich local food specialties. A unique
opportunity for an unforgettable holiday.

In addition to Skikjöring, gallop and harness racing,
St Moritz also has two other important equestrian events:
the historic *Concours Hippique de St. Moritz*, where horses
and riders compete in an obstacle course in the snow in an
almost surreal silence, and the Cartier Polo World Cup on
Snow, an international polo tournament that has been held
for over 25 years on the frozen lake. Every year, hundreds
of spectators attend this spectacular competition, which
is an absolute must in the calendar of international polo.
The importance of the event is highlighted by the famous
companies that finance the tournament, whose main sponsor
is Cartier, the well-known Swiss watchmaker.
Four teams from four different countries take part in the
tournament, which is of a very high standard. Each team is
made up of four players. Each player has to have six horses
to be able to cope with all the stages of the competition.
Polo is a very exciting game that leaves spectators
awestruck as they watch the acrobatic effort that the agile
horses exert to keep up with their competitors. Meanwhile,
the riders are engaged in trying to steal the ball from the
opposing team, to drive it into the opposing side's goal
with a bamboo mallet. There is no specific breed for
polo horses, but there is a preference for the Argentinian
Pony, considered to be better than any other horse in
this discipline and soon to be recognized as a breed.
The essential requirements of a polo pony are speed,
physical stamina, courage and good balance.

82-83 *St. Moritz has now been hosting the Cartier Polo World Cup on Snow,
an international polo tournament, for 25 years. Four teams take part. The players
of the French and German teams are in the picture.*

83 left *Polo horses have to be agile, skillful, courageous, balanced and calm
in addition to being very strong. The Argentinean Pony is the breed that has all
these qualities.*

83 right *Polo is exciting because of the extraordinary contortions the
horses skillfully go through to outwit their opponents. Acrobatic efforts
that sometimes end up in disastrous falls ...*

84-85 Cartier, the well-known Swiss watchmaker, has always been the main sponsor of the Polo World Cup on Snow, even taking part in the competition with its own team.

85 The game consists of trying to win the ball over from the opposing team, to drive it into the opposing side's goal with a bamboo mallet.

Symbol of a land

FRANCE ▪ BRITTANY

THE BRETON IS THE EMBLEM
OF THE FASCINATING LAND OF BRITTANY.

The Breton is a horse that has now acquired its own identity, even though the "Breton" name has long been given to all horses born and bred in Brittany in northwestern France. This breed has an ancient history and its evolution is complex. However, it is certain that it derives from the horse of the Montagnes Noires, a small, tough horse with a thick, black coat that descends from the mounts of the Celts. However, it is equally certain that the Breton's difference with respect to horses bred in other parts of Europe is the strong relationship it has established with the Breton people over years and years of working alongside each other. These conditions made it possible to develop animals of high quality and a thriving breeding and business practice.

By the Middle Ages, this region was a center of excellence for breeding working horses. Bretons are strong and tough, as well as distinguished and spirited, so they are excellent horses for all uses. The turning point for the definition of this breed, which became the main source of supply for Napoleon's army, came in 1806 when the emperor commissioned a reorganization of the *haras*, the French national centers for breeding and the improvement of breeds through the selection of stallions. One of these was located in the very center of the mountainous territory of Brittany, which says a great deal about the breeding vocation of this area.

Today, as in those days, the secret of the Breton's great success is its exceptional flexibility. Indeed, breeders in this region have always managed to meet market demands, adapting to varying requirements as they changed over time. And so, at different times, the Breton has been crossed with the powerful Boulonnais, Ardennes and Percheron horses, to increase its muscle mass and vigor for agricultural work, or with muscular English Norfolk Roadster stallions in order to obtain agile and fast draft horses for stagecoaches. Due to its outstanding qualities, the Breton, in turn, became a much sought-after horse to improve other draft breeds. Right up to the beginning of the last century, there was massive exportation not only to countries all over Europe but also to North Africa, the United States of America, South America and even Japan. And this was clearly a great contribution in support of the region's economy.

Today, the Breton is a national breed in France and two types are bred: one is the Trait Breton, a heavy, stocky, strong muscular horse that can exceed 163 cm (16 hands) in height at the withers with a weight of 900 kilograms. It is used mainly for the production of meat. The other is the Postier Breton, used as a light draft horse. With its lively gait, the Postier Breton is more distinguished but also smaller and lighter than the Trait Breton, from which it differs also because of its legs, which are virtually clean, with little or no feather. Both types come under the name of Breton (Bretone) and they are both registered in the same Stud Book that was officially founded in 1909. Because of its versatility and docility, in addition to its traditional uses in the artichoke and cauliflower fields, woods or vineyards, the Breton has now found a role in leisure activities, cutting a fine figure as a single draft horse but also in pairs or even quadrilles. It is also not at all unusual to see Bretons on feast days pulling carriages of cheerful families, or taking radiant brides to church. They are proud to participate in costume parades; attached to wagons, they even accompany tourists on holiday in the countryside.

BRITTANY

FRANCE

87 THE BRETON IS A HORSE THAT HAS LEFT ITS MARK ON THE DEVELOPMENT OF BRITTANY
IN NORTHWESTERN FRANCE. THE HORSES OF BRITTANY HAVE ALWAYS BEEN APPRECIATED
FOR WORK AND AS DRAFT HORSES.

88 NOWADAYS TWO TYPES OF BRETON HORSES ARE BRED. THEY ARE BOTH DESCENDED
FROM THE SMALL HORSES OF THE MONTAGNES NOIRES, WHICH, IN TURN, EXPERTS CONSIDER
TO BE THE DIRECT DESCENDANTS OF THE CELTS' HORSES.

89 A NUMBER OF OTHER BREEDS HAVE CONTRIBUTED TO THE DEVELOPMENT OF THE BRETON,
BREEDS LIKE THE MIGHTY BOULONNAIS, THE ARDENNES, THE PERCHERON AND EVEN THE
NORFOLK ROADSTER, AN AGILE, ENGLISH LIGHT DRAFT HORSE.

SAUMUR

FRANCE

The Cadre Noir de Saumur

FRANCE ▪ SAUMUR

THE "HIGH SCHOOL" EXERCISES EXECUTED BY THE HORSES
OF THE CADRE NOIR REQUIRE YEARS OF TRAINING.
THEIR SHOWS ARE THE STUFF OF DREAMS ...

Attending a show of the great masters of the *Ecole Nationale d'Equitation et du Cadre Noir de Saumur* (the French National Horse Riding School) engaged in "High School" exercises is exciting beyond all expectations. The origins of the Cadre Noir date back to 1832, when Charles X founded the *École Royale de Cavalerie*, now part of the *École Nationale d'Equitation* that works with the French Equestrian Federation, the *Haras Nationaux* (the so-called "National Studs," which are part of the French Horse and Horse Riding Institute) and the Ministry of Defense. Indeed, within this historic institution, the prestigious body of riding instructors, the *écuyers,* is divided into two sections, a military section and an academic section. The *écuyers* of the school of Saumur are the most famous French equestrian ambassadors in the world. They participate in all the major international equestrian events where they present the public with a series of "High School" displays that are unique in their genre. The choreography is original and studied in great detail. In addition to dressage, they practice all equestrian disciplines, at all levels, to disseminate the principles of classical French equitation.

The Cadre Noir School is located in Torrefort, 6 kilometers from the town of Saumur. The huge complex is composed of six Olympic-sized fields, a 40 km training track, a veterinary clinic, an amphitheater for conferences, five indoor riding school halls and 40 hectares of fields for young and retired horses.

The horses are bought at the age of 3 and, after an acclimatization period in the fields, they are housed in the stables, which can accommodate up to 360 horses, to be broken in and trained. Every year an average of 40 new horses are acquired, of which 10 percent are females. The horses are Anglo-Arabs coming exclusively from the Selle Français national breeding farm. The older horses, at the end of their careers in the school, are released to private individuals who adopt them, provide for their keep and look after them.

The Cadre Noir is composed of 45 civilians and military members grouped into *écuyers, sous-écuyers, maîtres* and *sous-maîtres.* It is directed by the *ecuyer en chef.* The school employs 200 people, including 60 grooms who look after the horses and prepare them for performances. The horses' manes and tails are braided with ribbons: reddish purple for horses reserved for riding exercises and white for jumpers that perform free jumping. In addition, there are five blacksmiths who hot-shoe 90 horses a week, using 5,000 horseshoes, 400 kilograms of nails and 12 tons of coal every year.

90-91 *The écuyers of the Saumur school, including some lady écuyeres, take part in the major equestrian events around the world with their spectacular exercises.*

90 *In the most difficult "airs," the horse leaps and all its limbs leave the ground. It takes years of training to achieve such results.*

92 *THE CHOREOGRAPHY OF EACH PERFORMANCE OF THE CADRE NOIR IS UNIQUE AND STUDIED IN MINUTE DETAIL. IN ADDITION TO DRESSAGE, THESE HORSES PRACTICE ALL THE OTHER EQUESTRIAN DISCIPLINES AT A VERY HIGH LEVEL.*

92-93 *THE HORSES ARE BOUGHT AT THE AGE OF 3 AND, AFTER AN ACCLIMATIZATION PERIOD IN THE FIELDS, THEY ARE HOUSED IN THE STABLES, WHICH CAN ACCOMMODATE UP TO 360 HORSES TO BE BROKEN IN AND TRAINED.*

FRANCE

PYRENEES

The King of the mountains

FRANCE ▪ PYRENEES

WITH THEIR TYPICAL BLACK COAT, THE MÉRENS LIVE IN THE WILD IN THE MOUNTAINS.

The mountains are the natural habitat of the Mérens, whose real name however is somewhat more high-sounding: Ariegeois. The *cheval ariégeois* or *cheval de Mérens* (two other names by which it is well known in France) owes its more common name to the small village in the Ariège department in the French Pyrenees on the border with the State of Andorra. The appearance of this sturdy little horse with its typical black coat betrays the influence of Arab stallions in its origins, but equally obvious is its resemblance to the prehistoric *chevaux Barbus* depicted in the cave of Niaux, dating back some 13,000 years, and the horses described by Julius Caesar in his *De bello gallico*. Regarding its deployment, due to its strength, reliability and remarkable ability to adapt to extreme conditions, since the Middle Ages the Mérens has been used extensively by military troops, agricultural workers in the mountains and miners transporting mineral ores. Much later, many of the horses used by Napoleon's troops in the Russian campaign were indeed *chevaux ariégeois*. After centuries of breeding and crossbreeding with different draft horses such as the Percheron and the Breton, the selective breeding of the Mérens, as we know it today, started in 1908 with individuals bred in the mountains on the border with Spain that were closer to their ancient ancestors. Subsequently, in 1948 the Stud Book was established and with it a whole series of tests and strict aptitude assessments (including working under the saddle, on long reins, harnessed and with cross-country obstacles) for stallions to be approved for public mating. Although Mérens horses today are bred practically all over Europe (and also in Tunisia!), they are still

essentially mountain horses. And it is the often hostile environment of the Pyrenees that has forged them over time. Much as they are hardy horses and great grazers, the Mérens eat only meadow grass and do not take willingly to being confined in stables. Indeed they prefer to live in the wild, in pastures in the mountains, until late fall. In winter, they descend to lower altitudes and it is only during snowbound periods that they are kept indoors. In the cold winter months, their coats become thicker with streaked rust-colored hair and facial features that look like beards, enabling them to face the inclement weather perfectly. Mérens learn to deal with the weather early in life when they are still colts. Indeed, when they are born in the spring, the pastures are still covered with snow. But Mérens colts grow quickly thanks to the remarkable lactating qualities of their mothers, and they also develop very quickly the unique characteristics of the breed, such as their adaptability and their resistance to the cold, their strong hooves, and their safe gaits even on nearly impenetrable mule tracks or along the edges of precipices. In addition, Mérens are also docile and strong, two characteristics that make them versatile and reliable for all uses. Mérens have always been employed in difficult agricultural work on terrains that are steep and impervious to such an extent that mechanization becomes inevitably limited. In these cases, they can often replace tractors. Indeed, Mérens today are highly appreciated for their versatility. Suitable as working horses, for combined driving and for pulling light loads such as sledges and tree trunks, Mérens have recently been successfully employed as riding horses for tourists engaged in mountain trekking, where their sure-footedness on steep trails makes them unbeatable.

94-95 LIKE MANY OTHER BREEDS OF HORSES, EVEN THE MÉRENS OWES ITS NAME TO A PLACE. IN THE CASE OF THIS RUGGED MOUNTAIN HORSE, IT IS A VILLAGE ON THE BORDER BETWEEN FRANCE AND ANDORRA IN THE FRENCH PYRENEES.

94 THE EXTREMELY TOUGH MÉRENS HORSES ARE BORN IN THE WILD. THEY GROW UP AND REPRODUCE IN ABSOLUTE FREEDOM IN THE MOUNTAINS, WHERE THEY FEED ON THE NUTRITIOUS GRASS OF THE PASTURES AT HIGH ALTITUDE. THEY STAY HERE FOR MOST OF THE YEAR, ALMOST UNTIL WINTER, WITHOUT SUFFERING ANY HARDSHIP.

FRANCE

CAMARGUE

The horses of the delta

FRANCE ■ CAMARGUE

IN THE MARSHES OF THE CAMARGUE, HORSES, BULLS AND WATERFOWL LIVE IN PERFECT SYMBIOSIS.

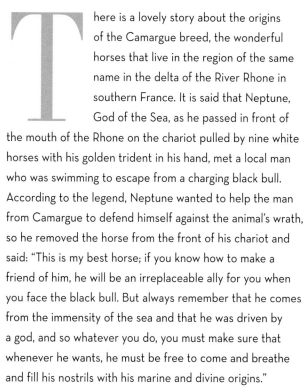

There is a lovely story about the origins of the Camargue breed, the wonderful horses that live in the region of the same name in the delta of the River Rhone in southern France. It is said that Neptune, God of the Sea, as he passed in front of the mouth of the Rhone on the chariot pulled by nine white horses with his golden trident in his hand, met a local man who was swimming to escape from a charging black bull. According to the legend, Neptune wanted to help the man from Camargue to defend himself against the animal's wrath, so he removed the horse from the front of his chariot and said: "This is my best horse; if you know how to make a friend of him, he will be an irreplaceable ally for you when you face the black bull. But always remember that he comes from the immensity of the sea and that he was driven by a god, and so whatever you do, you must make sure that whenever he wants, he must be free to come and breathe and fill his nostrils with his marine and divine origins."

And this is how the horse made its appearance in the Camargue, becoming one of its symbols. Of course, the true origin of these animals is quite different. They are probably the descendants of prehistoric horses whose remains have been discovered in abundance in Solutré, near Lyon. From prehistoric times to the present day, the Camargue horse has had to adapt to the difficult and inhospitable habitat of the wetlands of the Rhone delta, where it lives in the wild, spending much of its time in the marshes. And indeed this is

its essential characteristic, so much so that it was nicknamed "horse of the great river." It was Nature that forged this sturdy animal with strong legs, well suited for difficult terrain, and extremely hard hooves that are very resistant to humidity and very wide, so that the Camargue does not sink into the wet earth and is guaranteed safe and agile movement. Thanks to their "iron constitution," these horses have made the most of the meager resources that fate has dealt them, so much so that they manage to find sufficient sustenance where they live, in the poor marshy pastures swept by the strong cold northwesterly wind, a wind that in that part of the world has a fearsome name: the Mistral.

And so the Camargue horse has managed to survive by eating, most of the year, brackish grasses that it can graze on even under the surface of the water in the *sansouires* (the typical Camargue steppe) and the little vegetation, mostly burned by the sun, that sprouts in summer here and there between the arid cracks that appear in the dry land.

The horse's thick coat provides wonderful protection from the cold in winter, and from the horse flies and mosquitoes that infest the marshes in summer. There is even a reason for the color of its coat, dark as a colt and gray as an adult. In the former case the color ensures a good camouflage and therefore an added defense against predators, and in the latter case it constitutes the best protection against the scorching rays of the sun.

The Camargue horse is resistant, hardy, balanced, docile and calm, but at the same time vigorous. Thanks to its

96-97 *The charming Camargues live in the wild in the marshes of the Rhone Delta in southern France, the region which gave them their name.*

96 *The wonderful representatives of this breed have ancient origins: it is claimed that they are the direct descendants of the horses that lived in this region even in prehistoric times and that they have adapted, over the centuries, to the difficult conditions of the waterlogged environment.*

reliability, it is used as a herding horse and, more recently, has proved to be excellent for equestrian tourism as well as for a wide range of sports.

The Camargue is certainly a region that is well worth a visit, to see these unique horses and much more. There are many agritourism establishments that offer the possibility for splendid rambling in the Rhone Delta. The horses of the Camargue can now also be found elsewhere. For example, they have long been popular in Italy in the province of Ferrara and in all of Emilia Romagna. They were imported into this region, in the Po Delta, 20 years ago, and have adjusted perfectly, thanks to careful selection, to an environment that is less harsh than that of the Camargue and provides a more balanced diet. In order to set them apart from their French relatives, the horses that were born and bred in Italy are called Delta, as in Po Delta.

In addition to working equitation, in Italy the tireless and courageous Camargue-Delta excels in trekking and in other competitive sports, so much so that it is also deployed in reining, combined driving and vaulting. Thanks to its docility, it is also used for hippotherapy.

98 *THE CAMARGUE HORSES ARE ALSO KNOWN AS "SEA HORSES" AND IT IS NOT UNCOMMON TO SEE THEM RUNNING FREELY IN THE SHALLOW WATERS NEAR THE COAST, SPLASHING WITH THEIR POWERFUL LEGS.*

100 *The beautiful heads of these horses, with their wide flat foreheads, are surmounted by thick forelocks. Camargues have very sweet large eyes, endowed with considerable expressiveness. Their typical gray coat protects them from the heat of the sun.*

101 *The docile nature of the Camargue makes it particularly suitable for use in equestrian tourism and as a working horse. Many agritourism farms offer pleasure riding and trekking in the delta of the Rhone.*

102 TOP *The horses of this breed, which may seem quiet and almost sleepy when they are resting, can also be lively, agile and nimble, and often retain their boundless desire to frolic into adulthood, challenging each other playfully.*

102 BOTTOM *It is not uncommon to see white waterbirds that live in wetlands resting and relaxing on the wide solid backs of Camargue horses.*

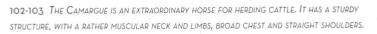

102-103 *The Camargue is an extraordinary horse for herding cattle. It has a sturdy structure, with a rather muscular neck and limbs, broad chest and straight shoulders.*

A festival in the name of the horse

FRANCE ■ AVIGNON

AVIGNON CELEBRATES THE NOBILITY OF THE HORSE
EVERY JANUARY WITH "CHEVAL PASSION."

For horse lovers, every year the season opens in Avignon with Cheval Passion. There is no enthusiast who has not heard of this event, one of the major European festivals of its kind, both in terms of numbers (over 1,200 horses, 14 arenas, 250 exhibitors and more than 100,000 spectators), and for its success in celebrating the horse as a noble animal that has always been close to man. Cheval Passion is one big show where everything is spectacular and artistic. And so, in January for five intense days, the Parc des Expositions in Avignon, the "city of the Popes" in the department of Vaucluse in Provence, becomes the undisputed capital of the horse and of horse riding. And every year it demonstrates that it is the most complete and attractive event of its kind in the equestrian world.

With each of its 26 editions, Cheval Passion has always glorified the bond that exists between horse and man and featured it as the main theme with respect to all the other activities –competitions, shows and exhibitions - that it presents. Unlike similar shows, however, the central theme of Cheval Passion is expressed not just through horse riding and sports, but with real passion as the show title suggests. Passion that

means tradition, intimacy, love, creativity and even a pure form of art. A passion shared by thousands of spectators who come to Cheval Passion and follow the packed program of events that includes over 90 hours of performances.

The pride of Cheval Passion is the *Gala des Crinières d'Or* (the Golden Mane Gala), an enchanting performance set in a fairy tale atmosphere, somewhere between myth and legend, that stages horses, comedians, musicians and riders. Year after year, the gala manages to attract the best equestrian artists of the time. The first *Gala des Crinières d'Or* was staged during the first Cheval Passion in 1986, and during its 26 editions it has featured over 300 equestrian acts - many of them performed for the first time - that have since been shown around the world. Cheval Passion is also an exhibition of horse breeds and of breeding farms. Here again, the horses are not displayed in the classical fashion; the horses themselves show off their aptitudes and potential in the course of brief performances, competitions, exhibitions, special category events such as "Pony Passion" and much more. There are also days dedicated to education and training, for example, vocational training in the equestrian sector. And this is another reason why Cheval Passion has become an undisputed point of reference in the world of horses and equestrian shows.

104 *MANY COUNTRIES HAVE AT LEAST ONE FESTIVAL THAT IS DEDICATED TO HORSES AND THEIR WORLD. FRANCE WITH CHEVAL PASSION BOASTS ONE OF THE MOST FASCINATING AND INTERNATIONALLY RENOWNED HORSE FESTIVALS.*

105 *CHEVAL PASSION HAS NOW REACHED ITS 26TH EDITION AND EVERY YEAR IT HAS A RICH PROGRAM FULL OF TOP CLASS EQUESTRIAN PERFORMANCES, INCLUDING SOME THAT ARE PRESENTED TO THE PUBLIC FOR THE FIRST TIME.*

FRANCE

AVIGNON ●

106 *The Horse Festival in Avignon is one of the most visited in the world and culminates with the Gala des Crinières d'Or. Year after year, the Gala attracts the best equestrian artists of the time.*

106-107 *For horse lovers, Cheval Passion is a once-in-a-lifetime must. This great event is in fact one of the few that highlight the intimate relationship between man and horse.*

The horses from Lusitania

PORTUGAL

THE LUSITANO IS PROUD AND COURAGEOUS IN THE ARENA, BUT GRACEFUL AND ELEGANT IN "HIGH SCHOOL" EQUESTRIANISM.

For centuries, Iberian horses were the most coveted horses of kings, leaders and generals, who chose them for their grandeur, beauty, docility, strength and courage. They have always been selected to fight against men and bulls and to perform in "High School" displays. One of the fine horses bred on the Iberian Peninsula is the Lusitano. It may be a little less striking than its better-known and much-lauded Andalusian "cousin," but its exceptional courage has enabled it to gain fame and success. Historically, the Iberian horse has long been identified more generally as Spanish or Andalusian, including horses such as the Lusitanos. Even though they essentially belong to the same breed, however, they have an autonomous development that is linked to the Portuguese equestrian tradition and in particular to bullfighting.

Portuguese bullfights, where the Lusitanos perform, have developed differently from those in Spain. In the arenas of Portugal, the protagonists have always been the *rejoneadores.* who are *toreadores* on horseback. This resulted in the first distinction between the Iberian horses bred in the two areas, helping to forge a fundamental characteristic of the Lusitano: courage. It is impressive to see one of these horses fearlessly facing an angry bull, as the horse and its rider gallop straight toward it, avoiding the bull's fearsome horns with an agile elegant swerve at the very last moment. It is not by chance that the Portuguese bullfight does not end with the killing of the bull and is considered a real art.

In the last century, equestrian art was made famous throughout the world by the famous rider and horseman Nuno Oliveira, who, with his Lusitanos, was able to transform academic riding into art.

The modern history of this horse is, however, quite recent. It was only in the 1960s that the Portuguese breeders created their Stud Book, giving a definitive identity and dignity to their horses that have been called Lusitanos since 1966. The name derives from the Roman name for Portugal, Lusitania. Bullfights and courage apart, the versatility and obedience of the Lusitano are the perfect qualities to facilitate training for working with herds of bulls under the saddle of the *campinos* and in dressage or "High School" performance.

Thanks to their qualities, Lusitanos are currently among the leaders on the international scene in *doma vaquero*, which has now become a true sporting discipline derived from working equitation, and in dressage at the highest competitive levels, while the "High School" tradition is maintained by the Escola Portuguesa de Arte Equestre. For their performances, the riders of the Escola all mount Lusitano stallions that were bred on the Alter Real State Stud Farm, founded in 1748 by King João V. Alter Real horses, as horses that are born there are called, are the result of selective breeding to produce horses of exceptional quality, suitable for classical "High School" but also to pull the carriages of the royal court of Lisbon. When the Portuguese monarchy was abolished, the breeding of the Alter-Real strain came to an end, but fortunately Ruy d'Andrade, a great horseman, managed to save a small group of horses from which he selected two stallions that carried on the selective breeding of these horses, the pride of Portuguese equine heritage.

PORTUGAL

108-109 THE LUSITANO IS A "COUSIN" OF THE BETTER-KNOWN ANDALUSIAN. THE BREED, HOWEVER, WAS DEVELOPED INDEPENDENTLY IN PORTUGAL, AND TODAY THIS HORSE IS KNOWN AND APPRECIATED ALL OVER THE WORLD FOR ITS SPECIAL QUALITIES.

110 *The Lusitano's coat is predominantly gray. Among the typical characteristics of the breed, pride and courage are the most obvious and the most widely appreciated.*

111 *Lusitano horses are not lacking in beauty. They have an imposing presence, they are solid, they are characterized by elegance of form and movement and, like all Iberian horses, they boast long flowing manes.*

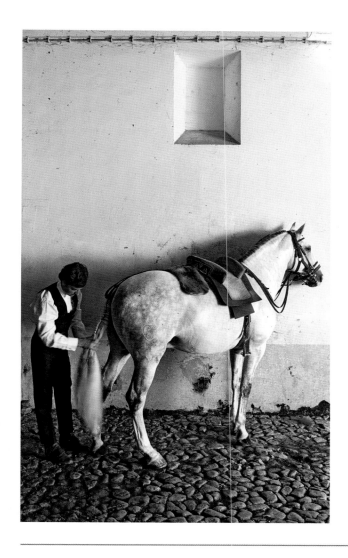

112-113 *The Lusitano is an extremely versatile horse. A working horse used for herding cattle and performing in the doma vaquera sports discipline, it also excels as a horse for country riding.*

113 *In Portugal the horse is an integral part of the national culture. Indeed, there is a deep and sincere relationship between man and this splendid animal; their friendship thrives as the result of daily care and attention.*

114-115 *The Lusitano horse is the product of the Portuguese equestrian tradition that has brought to the fore, together with the horse, the figure of the rejoneador, the mounted toreador, and the picador, the horseman with the pica or lance.*

Dancing horses

SPAIN ▪ JEREZ DE LA FRONTERA

JEREZ DE LA FRONTERA IS THE HOME OF THE *REAL ESCUELA* AND SPLENDID ANDALUSIAN HORSES.

The *Real Escuela Andaluza del Arte Ecuestre* (Royal Andalusian School of Equestrian Art) in Jerez de la Frontera is one of the most important institutions in the world, committed to pass on the dictates of "High School" equestrianism and keep up the centuries-old history of the art of horse riding and of the Andalusian horse. The first horse show to be held in Jerez was in the 17th century at the behest of Don Bruno de Morla Melgarejo. Subsequently, in 1738 Don Bruno published an essay, the *Libro nuevo de bueltas escaramuza, de gala a la gineta*, which has since become the reference text book for classical equitation, where "collection" is considered to be the ultimate in horse balance.

Centuries of tradition in the art of High School equitation and in breeding prized Andalusians have now found a sublime and natural homecoming in the birth of the Royal Andalusian School of Equestrian Art. The Real Escuela, one of the most renowned in the world for High School Equitation, was founded in 1973 by Don Álvaro Romero Domecq. And it was thanks to Don Álvaro, one of the greatest *rejoneador* of all time, that Spain has regained its former glory in equestrian art. Initially, the Real Escuela, which was granted a Royal Charter in 1987 by King Juan Carlos, was developed under the direct management of its creator, but subsequently the Spanish Ministry of Information and Tourism took over

the institution. A palace was acquired to house the Real Escuela in Jerez de la Frontera, the Recreo de las Cadenas, a 19th century palace with a large park, designed in the Renaissance style with subtle baroque overtones by architect Charles Garnier, who designed the Paris Opera House.

Don Álvaro Romero Domecq was appointed director of the Real Escuela Andaluza del Arte Ecuestre. It has since extended the premises, adding, in 1980, an arena that can accommodate up to 1,600 spectators and stables that can house 60 horses. For the preservation of equestrian tradition, in 1986 the Real Escuela acquired the stables of Don Pedro Domecq de la Riva, including their fine Spanish breed horses, and above all an invaluable collection of 19 carriages together with saddles and bridles of immense historical value, some of them dating as far back as 1730.

The shows, which feature all the High School routines, the displays with the spectacular Spanish gait of the Andalusian horses and the international tours of the Real Escuela Andaluza del Arte Ecuestre are just some of the many activities of this institution, which is an important social and cultural ambassador of the Spanish equestrian heritage. Indeed, the Real Escuela has also contributed to the selective breeding of Andalusian horses that are used for High School exercises and dressage, and is involved in the training of the riders.

116-117 TWO HORSEMEN FROM THE REAL ESCUELA ANDALUZA DEL ARTE ECUESTRE LEAD THEIR NOBLE STEEDS THROUGH THE LAVISH CORRIDORS OF THE PRESTIGIOUS SPANISH INSTITUTION, FOUNDED AND DIRECTED BY DON ÁLVARO DOMECQ ROMERO, ONE OF THE GREATEST REJONEADORES IN HISTORY.

117 THE REAL ESCUELA WAS FOUNDED IN 1973 IN JEREZ DE LA FRONTERA, WITH HEADQUARTERS IN THE RECREO DE LAS CADENAS, AN ANCIENT PALACE BUILT IN THE 18TH CENTURY RENAISSANCE STYLE, TO WHICH STABLES AND AN ARENA WERE SUBSEQUENTLY ADDED.

SPAIN

JEREZ DE LA FRONTERA

118 TOP *The horses of this prestigious institution are all magnificent Andalusian stallions, which are regularly mounted daily by professional riders to complete their long training.*

118 BOTTOM *Thanks to the exceptional performances in Jerez de la Frontera, but above all because of the tours and the exhibitions that are held abroad, the Real Escuela Andaluza del Arte Ecuestre is one of the undisputed symbols of equestrian "High School" in the world.*

118-119 *One of the duties of the Real Escuela in Jerez de la Frontera is to select the horses to be used in the High School displays and in dressage, in addition to training male and female riders.*

120 *THE PERFORMANCES FEATURE ONLY THE BEAUTIFUL ANDALUSIAN STALLIONS (NOW CALLED PRE, PURA RAZA ESPAÑOLA). THE BEST HORSES ALSO COMPETE IN DRESSAGE COMPETITIONS OF THE HIGHEST INTERNATIONAL STANDARDS.*

120-121 *THE PERFORMANCES OF THE REAL ESCUELA ANDALUZA DEL ARTE ECUESTRE ALWAYS ATTRACT THOUSANDS OF SPECTATORS. INDEED, THERE ARE MANY TOURISTS WHO VISIT JEREZ DE LA FRONTERA FOR THE SOLE PURPOSE OF ATTENDING THE EXTRAORDINARY EQUESTRIAN EXHIBITIONS.*

122 *The training of a horse is long and very laborious, and requires great skill. Indeed, not all the horses have the superior qualities necessary to perform the more demanding and difficult High School routines.*

123 *Groundwork is one of the most interesting parts of the program of the Real Escuela shows. This includes the so-called "airs," amongst which there is the spectacular levade.*

La Feria de Abril

SPAIN ▪ SEVILLE

EVERY YEAR IN APRIL, SEVILLE IS THE SCENE OF ONE OF THE FINEST EQUESTRIAN EVENTS IN THE WORLD.

The Feria de Abril was once a livestock fair but today it is one of the best-known folkloric nonreligious festivals in Andalusia, the southernmost region in Spain. It is known around the world, in particular for its undisputed protagonist: the Pure Spanish horse. La Feria de Abril in Seville is usually held in April, although falling one or two weeks after Easter means that it can also take place in early May. The first festival was held in 1847 in the Prado de San Sebastian, while the current fair takes place in the neighborhood called Los Remedios. The festival started as a way to overcome the dark period of Lent and to alleviate the daily concerns of the inhabitants of the city.

Today the Feria de Abril is a veritable feast of fun, joy and friendship. On the days of the Fair, the whole city comes to a halt. The shops close, and at midnight on Monday, the feast begins with the *Alumbrado*, the evocative lighting of the lamps of the fair enclosure (the Real) and the thousands of light bulbs of the *portada*, the main gate of the Feria enclosure. The party continues until the following Sunday, when it ends with a magnificent fireworks display.

Every day of the entire week of celebrations, about 3,000 riders and 600 carriages enter the *Recinto Ferial* from noon until eight o'clock in the evening. Men on horseback, in carriages and on foot parade through the streets, singing and dancing ... The splendid horses are harnessed in the traditional Andalusian style, called *calesera*, flaunting neckbands of bells, the *cascabeles*, and the characteristic two-tone ornamental pompons, the *borlajes*. Even the horses ridden by men and women are harnessed and groomed with great care and elegance, showing off the perfect colorful decorations in their flowing manes and tails.

124-125 *THE THEATER IS BEAUTIFUL SEVILLE, THE SHOW IS ONE OF THE MOST IMPORTANT FESTIVALS IN ANDALUSIA AND THE UNDISPUTED STAR IS THE PURA RAZA ESPAÑOLA (PURE SPANISH BREED).*

125 *AS ITS NAME SUGGESTS, THE FERIA DE ABRIL USUALLY TAKES PLACE IN APRIL. THE FAIR STARTED IN 1847 AND CURRENTLY TAKES PLACE IN THE DISTRICT OF LOS REMEDIOS.*

SPAIN

SEVILLE

126 ORIGINALLY CREATED TO OVERCOME THE DARK PERIOD OF LENT, TODAY IT IS A FESTIVAL THAT IS FULL OF FUN, FRIENDSHIP AND SINGING. THE WHOLE CITY STOPS AND EVERYONE JOINS IN THE FUN IN ELEGANT TRADITIONAL ANDALUSIAN COSTUMES.

126-127 ON FOOT, ON HORSEBACK OR IN CARRIAGES, EVERYBODY PARADES THROUGH THE CITY. EVERY DAY OF THE ENTIRE WEEK OF CELEBRATIONS, ABOUT 3,000 RIDERS AND 600 CARRIAGES ENTER THE RECINTO FERIAL.

128-129 *In the arena of the Maestranza, where bullfighting takes place in the afternoon, there is a parade with riders and horse-drawn carriages all decorated in the traditional Andalusian style, with collars of bells (cascabeles) and two-tone pompons (borlajes).*

129 *The beautiful horses are well-groomed and they look very elegant with braided manes and tails and immaculate, shining trappings.*

130-131 *Menorquinas are the undisputed protagonists of the fiestas that take place on their island of origin. Proud and fully conscious of their role, these horses advance unperturbed through the crowded streets and squares.*

131 *The most important event of Menorca is the Fiesta de Sant Joan. Every year on 23 and 24 June, Ciutadella returns to the past and for two whole days it is full of horses adorned with precious decorations.*

132-133 *Menorquinas are horses of great intelligence, and they demonstrate their versatility when their skill, and that of their riders, is put to the test during the various festivals in which they take part.*

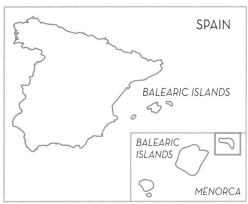

SPAIN

BALEARIC ISLANDS

BALEARIC ISLANDS

MENORCA

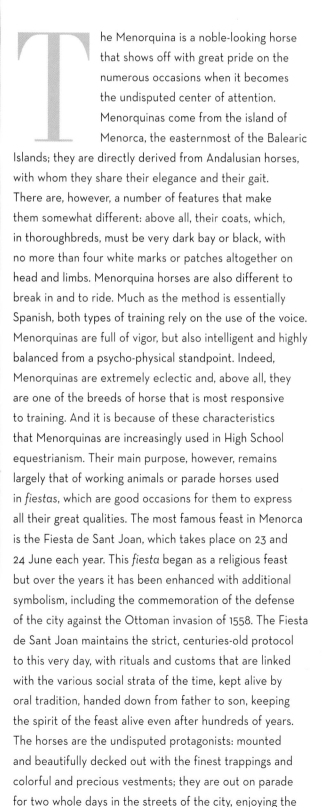

At the center of the fiesta

SPAIN ▪ MENORCA

THE MENORQUINA HORSE IS THE STAR OF THE FIESTA DE SANT JOAN ON THE ISLAND OF MENORCA.

The Menorquina is a noble-looking horse that shows off with great pride on the numerous occasions when it becomes the undisputed center of attention. Menorquinas come from the island of Menorca, the easternmost of the Balearic Islands; they are directly derived from Andalusian horses, with whom they share their elegance and their gait. There are, however, a number of features that make them somewhat different: above all, their coats, which, in thoroughbreds, must be very dark bay or black, with no more than four white marks or patches altogether on head and limbs. Menorquina horses are also different to break in and to ride. Much as the method is essentially Spanish, both types of training rely on the use of the voice. Menorquinas are full of vigor, but also intelligent and highly balanced from a psycho-physical standpoint. Indeed, Menorquinas are extremely eclectic and, above all, they are one of the breeds of horse that is most responsive to training. And it is because of these characteristics that Menorquinas are increasingly used in High School equestrianism. Their main purpose, however, remains largely that of working animals or parade horses used in *fiestas*, which are good occasions for them to express all their great qualities. The most famous feast in Menorca is the Fiesta de Sant Joan, which takes place on 23 and 24 June each year. This *fiesta* began as a religious feast but over the years it has been enhanced with additional symbolism, including the commemoration of the defense of the city against the Ottoman invasion of 1558. The Fiesta de Sant Joan maintains the strict, centuries-old protocol to this very day, with rituals and customs that are linked with the various social strata of the time, kept alive by oral tradition, handed down from father to son, keeping the spirit of the feast alive even after hundreds of years. The horses are the undisputed protagonists: mounted and beautifully decked out with the finest trappings and colorful and precious vestments; they are out on parade for two whole days in the streets of the city, enjoying the greatest respect, and also the right of way which everyone must concede to them by at any time. On these occasions, all the excitement and warmth of the crowd are unleashed, but the horses remain composed and collected and as proud as ever, proceeding with ease, making their way through the crowd that fills the streets. On these occasions, Menorquinas seem to be perfectly aware of their role and that they are the center of everybody's attention. As if by magic, however, they respond to their riders' imperceptible commands and, every now and then, they turn around in a figure-8 that forces spectators to step back to a safe distance. Having made space for themselves in this manner, they will then perform a *levade*, a very challenging and spectacular High School exercise. The best trainers and riders perform the exercise without using their hands, deliberately dropping the reins on the horses' necks. The horses stay in this position, on their hind legs, for a considerable length of time, amid the admiration of the spectators and with the riders taking pride in their own and their horses' talent.

The Blond Mountain horse

ITALY ■ AVELENGO

THE AVELIGNESE IS THE KING OF THE ITALIAN MOUNTAINS.
THE BREED IS MORE THAN 100 YEARS OLD AND IS FOUND THROUGHOUT
ITALY, AUSTRIA, GERMANY AND MANY OTHER COUNTRIES IN EUROPE.

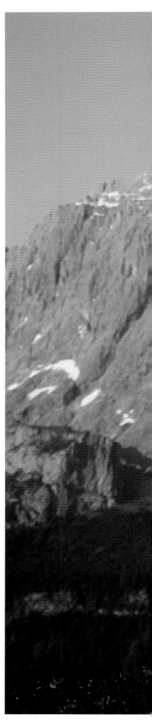

It is a small horse, so much so that it is sometimes called a pony. It is hardy enough to survive without any problems in the mountains and, above all, it is versatile. The Avelignese is a breed which, as the name suggests, traces its origins back to Avelengo (Hafling), a small town near Merano in Alto Adige. The Aveglinese, which is also known by its German name, Haflinger, is a medium-size, well-balanced horse with a sturdy but graceful build and an elegant bearing. To complete this little "masterpiece" of Nature, the Aveglinese has an attractive chestnut, or preferably golden coat, and a long pale gold mane and tail. All these features make the Avelignese extremely pleasing to behold, as well as to ride on all types of terrain. Quiet, loyal, obedient, with a confident gait, the Haflinger can also be lively and brave, but the secrets of its success are essentially its incredible docility, making for easy handling even by the elderly, women and children, and its remarkable aptitude for learning. These two qualities make it an irreplaceable companion for sharing a multitude of activities. Indeed, it is used in the various riding disciplines, from English Riding to Western Riding, in harness racing, and even in Skikjöring, a galloping race in the snow pulling a skier.

The Avelignese is an eclectic horse and it is perfect for teaching riding. Many riding schools use it for riding lessons and hippotherapy, a riding practice with an important social value. But this versatility should not obscure its origins; for over a century the Avelignese was selected and bred for farming and mountain transport, activities that, even in today's hyper-mechanized world, are jealously guarded and kept alive for the sake of tradition by farmers in South Tyrol. The strong and sturdy Haflinger, endowed with great versatility, can withstand the rigors of life in the open, such as harsh climates and sparse meals, relatively easily. It is also for this reason that breeding farms are set up in wild areas. This horse is calm and obedient, strong and robust, and it is suitable for long walks in the mountains or in high hilly areas. It is the ideal traveling companion for riding in the countryside and trekking, even on difficult terrain at high altitudes, in woods and along steep paths where sure-footedness is essential. It is recommended for small children and less experienced riders and is the perfect horse for a first riding experience.

Today, the Haflinger is found all over Europe (particularly in Austria, where breeding is thriving) and also in other countries around the world. It is the most numerous horse breed in Italy, where it can be found in virtually all regions. Much as the Haflinger can now be found all over the world, it is undeniable that it is precisely in its homeland that it is used in the best and most varied ways, and not only in daily tasks or sports and leisure activities. Indeed, in South Tyrol there is no feast, festival or event where the blond horses are not the undisputed protagonists. For a breeder, showing off his Haflinger decked out in its Sunday best is a way of saying "thank you" for all the times that it has been strong, patient and humble in its daily work. This is also a sign of the ancestral link between mountain people and their inseparable companion over the centuries.

The calendar of Haflinger events is very rich, ranging from folkloric parades with all the traditional trappings to races with sledges and Skikjöring. Among the most important events is the *Slittada da paur*, which means "Farmers' Sleigh Run" in the local Ladin language. This traditional annual horse-drawn sleigh parade takes place on Carnival Sunday in Alta Badia in the heart of the Dolomites. It departs from the resort of Pedraces and proceeds to the center of La Villa. The event's high point is a sleigh race, at a trot, over a distance of 400 meters.

Moreover, every year in November, there is the traditional San Leonardo horse ride. This is a procession organized in honor of the patron saint of farmers, prisoners, slaves, blacksmiths and carpenters. Representatives from all four Ladin valleys take part in the procession in San Leonardo, Alta Badia, in traditional costumes. The Haflingers, looking splendid in their trappings, are always a great attraction!

AVELENGO   ITALY

134-135 THE AVELIGNESE, WHOSE ORIGINAL NAME IN TYROLEAN DIALECT IS HAFLINGER,
IS ORIGINALLY FROM AVELENGO, OR HAFLING IN GERMAN, A SMALL TOWN NEAR MERANO
IN ALTO ADIGE.

136 *The Haflinger, now widespread all over Europe, easily withstands living outdoors. Indeed, Haflingers are always bred in the wild.*

137 *Born and raised on rough and mountainous terrain, Haflingers learn from an early age to move with sure steps as they play together.*

138-139 *The most noticeable features of these strong sturdy horses are their golden chestnut coat and their long, thick blond mane, which they show off with pride.*

The pride of Italy

ITALY ■ MAREMMA

OF ALL THE BREEDS OF ITALIAN HORSES, THE MAREMMANO IS THE ONE THAT HAS MANAGED TO MAINTAIN ITS IDENTITY.

There are few areas in Italy where the bond between man and horse is as strong as in Maremma. And it was this exceptional bond, fostered by day after day of hard work with the Butteri (Tuscan cowboys) and their cattle, that has made the Maremmano, which is the only native Italian saddle horse breed, together with its riders, the symbol of a land. The first definition of a Maremmano horse dates back to a written account from the 16th century, but the breed originated in the times of the ancient Etruscans, who occupied the territories now called Maremma in present-day Tuscany and northern Latium. Until the middle of the last century, Maremma was an unhealthy, inhospitable and windswept swamp where the famous long-horned Maremma cattle and the horses were raised in the wild. They were recurring themes, along with the Butteri, in the paintings of Giovanni Fattori. The extreme conditions of the habitat and the shortage of food contributed, little by little, to the definition of a small, rather unattractive but extremely useful horse with a strong temperament, which was both strong and flexible. In past centuries, various cavalries helped themselves to horses bred in the Maremma. The Savoy army was able to rely on the endurance of these horses in various war campaigns, including the Crimean War of 1855-56. The state, through the army, continued to be the major buyer of these horses for a long time, up to the first half of the last century. However, in the 1950s, increased mechanization,

the Land Reform and the allotment of large estates, which came about as a result of land reclamation, brought the Maremmano to the brink of extinction. The glorious old stud farms were dismantled and many mares were mated with Rapid Heavy Draft horses to obtain foals for meat. However, the bond between man and his animals was too strong and, little by little, the horses reappeared in the Maremma. A group of breeders then began to search the countryside around Rome and Viterbo for any surviving Maremmani. Provincial associations of breeders were founded in Viterbo and Grosseto in the late 1960s, and in 1972 they joined their efforts to determine the number of surviving horses. In 1979 the Association of the Breed was founded and the Stud Book was created the following year. It is therefore thanks to the breeders of Tuscany and Latium that the Maremmano was able to recover its identity and secure its future.

Whereas its main vocation remains that of a faithful working companion of the Butteri, the Maremmano is now a riding horse that is used in all walks of life. Thanks to its docility, its sure-footedness, its great strength and its ability to adapt to different situations, it is appreciated in country equitation and equestrian tourism. Moreover, because of its versatility, it is also able to achieve remarkable results even in sporting competitions. Many excellent results have been obtained by Maremmani in almost all sports disciplines, including working equitation, a specialty where they excel thanks to their easy handling and reliability that have been refined over dozens of years of working with livestock.

140-141 *The Butteri (Tuscan cowboys) and their Maremmani are the symbols of an extraordinary land. In this area, the bond between man and horse is unique, the product of years of a shared life of hard work.*

141 *The Maremmano is the only native Italian saddle breed. Even though its origins are ancient, selective breeding began only in 1979 with the foundation of the Associazione di Razza (Breed Association) followed by the creation of a Stud Book.*

ITALY

MAREMMA

142-143 *The Maremma has always been an area with a strong breeding tradition. In addition to horses, Maremma cattle, with their easily recognizable long horns, are also raised here in the wild.*

144-145 *In a land of great tradition like Maremma, life is punctuated by rhythms dictated by nature. One of these is the weaning of cattle that are separated from their mothers by the Butteri on horseback.*

146 *The Butteri tame and train their horses themselves. After an initial taming phase, the colts are immediately mounted at work in the country, together with older and more skilled horses.*

146-147 *The traditional method for breeding the Maremmano Horse is that of the razzetta, with groups of mares living in semi-liberty with a stallion, which is placed in the herd in the spring.*

An appointment with history

ITALY ▪ SIENA

WITH ALMOST 1,000 YEARS OF HISTORY BEHIND IT, THE PALIO DI SIENA IS NOW STAGED TWICE A YEAR.

The date of its origin is not certain, but there is no doubt that the history of the nearly 1,000-year-old Palio is very closely related to history of the city that hosts it. Indeed, the Palio di Siena is not a simple re-enactment. The Palio itself is history, history that repeats itself continuously as it has done for centuries. "Il Palio è dei senesi" (The Palio belongs to the people of Siena), it is said, confirming that the origins of the race are deeply embedded in the culture of the city. It is a true popular festival, deep-rooted in the community of Siena, which participates in the activities of the local *contrade* (city neighborhood) all year round. But the Palio is so unique and spectacular that it also attracts thousands of tourists from all over the world. Tourists dive into the kaleidoscope of colors in Piazza del Campo, where horses and riders – who ride their horses bareback, that is, without a saddle – go to meet their destiny, galloping three times around the square.

The Palio has very remote origins. Indeed, as early as the Middle Ages in Siena there were numerous *carriere*, as the races were then called, organized by the nobility on the occasion of feasts, in honor of saints and for the celebration of special events. One of these was dedicated to the Assumption in mid-August. This race was subsequently formalized in 1310 with an entry in the Municipal Charter. However, these races were different from the current Palio, as they were run in *alla lunga* fashion, meaning that they started at one point in the city and ran across it to a finishing point. The prize was what, in Latin, is called a *pallium*, a banner of precious fabric with an image of the coat of arms of the rulers of the city. It was only in the 18th century that it became customary for this image to be painted on the banner. The oldest one to be preserved in Siena is in the museum of the Contrada of the Eagle and it dates back to 2 July, 1719. The horses were ridden by young jockeys dressed in the colors of the great noble families. Later they started to have the horses run without jockeys, decked with plumes, rosettes or caparisons to identify them. Meanwhile, the passion of the people of Siena had turned to the races that the *contrade* had organized in *alla tonda* fashion, i.e., laps around a track, in Piazza del Campo, since the 17th century. These races, organized by the *contrade*

148 *The crest of the Contrada of the She-Wolf stands out on the flag. The Palio di Siena is much more than just a horse race; it is a piece of history that repeats itself in July and again in August, and it involves the whole community of Siena all year round.*

149 *Ten contrade (districts) participate in the Palio di Siena. Seven of them are entitled to participate; they are the ones that did not run in the same Palio (in July or August) the previous year. The other three are selected by drawing lots.*

ITALY

SIENA

- and therefore by the people, and not the nobility - are what evolved into the Palio as we know it today.

In 1656 the City of Siena decided to take over the organization of the Palio of 2 July, dedicated to the Madonna of Provenzano and linked to an incident that occurred during the Spanish and Florentine occupation of Siena at the end of the 16th century. The first records of the race date back to 1659, even though it existed before that date, and it is from that year onward that the "official" victories of the districts have been recorded. Beginning in 1701, on 16 August each year the *contrade* organized the Palio dell'Assunta (the Palio of the Assumption) and the race was run around the Piazza del Campo. After the abolition of the Palios that were run *alla lunga* by the City of Siena in 1874, the Palio dell'Assunta was the only Palio to be held, in addition to the one of 2 July. Another fundamental development in the modern history of the Palio dates back to 1729, when the Governor of Siena, Violante di Bavaria, established the boundaries of the *contrade*, and also decreed, for security reasons, that not more than 10 *contrade* could participate in any single race. And so, of the 17 city *contrade* into which Siena is divided, seven are entitled to participate, with a horse that is assigned to them by drawing lots: the *contrade* that are entitled to run are those who did not run in the same Palio (2 July or 16 August) the previous year. The other three are chosen by lots, thus keeping alive a tradition that has existed for centuries, a tradition that is renewed year after year with the customary starting procedure known as *mossa* between the starting ropes.

150-151 *The cavalry charge of the mounted Carabinieri in the Piazza del Campo is one of many moments that enrich the historic Palio di Siena.*

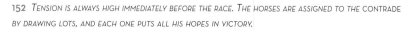

152 TENSION IS ALWAYS HIGH IMMEDIATELY BEFORE THE RACE. THE HORSES ARE ASSIGNED TO THE CONTRADE BY DRAWING LOTS, AND EACH ONE PUTS ALL HIS HOPES IN VICTORY.

152-153 ALTHOUGH THE ASSIGNMENT OF THE HORSE IS TOTALLY UNKNOWN AND IS ALMOST CONSIDERED A SIGN OF DESTINY, EACH CONTRADA MEMBER HAS A PROFOUND AND SINCERE AFFECTION FOR THE ANIMAL THAT IS ASSIGNED TO HIS CONTRADA BY CHANCE, AND BECOMES THE OBJECT OF RESPECT AND ADMIRATION.

154-155 *The Palio comes to a climax with the race itself. The race goes three times around the Piazza del Campo and once they set off, the horses and jockeys go at full gallop amidst the screams of thousands of spectators who fill the square.*

155 TOP *One of the tensest moments of the Palio is the entry of the horses between the canapi, the two ropes that delimit the area of the mossa (starting procedures): the order of call is also determined by drawing lots and announced by the starter at the last minute.*

155 *The horses are the true protagonists of the race in Piazza del Campo, as a horse can confer the victory on its contrada by reaching the finishing line first even if it has lost its jockey.*

Sa Sartiglia

ITALY ▪ ORISTANO

EVERY YEAR IN SARDINIA, THE TOWN OF ORISTANO IS THE SCENE
OF A SPECTACULAR EVENT, CELEBRATED DURING CARNIVAL,
WHICH BODES AN AUSPICIOUS BEGINNING OF SPRING.

For more than 500 years, on Carnival Sunday and the following Tuesday, the ancient feast of the *Sartiglia* is celebrated in Oristano, Sardinia. An event that evokes a spectacularly real medieval tournament and, at the same time, reenacts the symbolism of an auspicious and propitiatory rite: a star with a hole in its center through which riders have to insert their swords or a wooden lance, symbolizing the earth that must be made fertile so it will bear fruit. The *Sartiglia*, which has its roots in the chivalrous equestrian tournaments of medieval Europe, at the time of the Crusades, is one of the most spectacular folkloric events and, above all, one of the most passionate of Sardinian culture. It is a celebration of a thousand and one symbols. Symbols of magic and prosperity but also of poverty, pain and hope.

During the *Sartiglia* the city of Oristano comes to a halt and fills with music, color, people wearing fascinating disguises, but above all, horses ... Indeed, 120 riders take part in the *Sartiglia*, split into teams of three, for a total of 40 so-called *pariglias*. The horses are born and bred in Sardinia, a land with an ancient equestrian tradition. These horses are very spirited, athletic, agile and alert with ancient and noble Arab blood in their veins: the ancestry of the Anglo-Arabian breed of Sardinia, a strong and courageous horse, the pride of the island's breeders and riders. The horses go through a long physical training program throughout the whole year. This training prepares them to face the challenges of the *Sartiglia* in the best possible way so they complete it full of positive energy, without any difficulties. The protagonists of the *pariglie* race are often the small and agile Giara Horses from the Sardinian Giara plateau.

Two horsemen, called the *Componidori*, are appointed to supervise the two contests, one on Sunday and one on Tuesday. It is the high dignitaries of the two *gremios*, the ancient trade guilds, who nominate the *componidori*: the farmers' *gremio* nominates the *Componidori* for the Sunday contest while the carpenters' *gremio* nominates the one for the contest on Tuesday. The *Componidori* robing ritual, which lasts a whole morning, is rich in symbolic meaning. When the *Componidori* is finally ready, he is given a horse to mount. Amid a roar of applause and cheering the *Componidori* goes out into the square on horseback to greet and bless all those present. With his two *pariglia* companions, he goes to the parvis of the cathedral of Santa Maria Assunta from where the long-awaited star contest runs will start. The event unfolds along the Via del Duomo, covered with sand

156 *The festival derives its name from the Castilian* sortija, *which in turn comes from the Latin* sorticola (*diminutive of* sors, *meaning "good fortune"), and which also means "ring." The tournament in fact belongs to the so-called "running at the rings" category.*

for the occasion, and just below the bell tower of the cathedral a green ribbon is strung across, with the prized target, the tin star, in the middle.

The contest is now open! The first one to try his skill is the *Componidori* himself, who sets off at a gallop, followed by his two aides-de-camp, with his lance thrust forward ready to "pierce" the star. After the *Componidori*'s attempt, the other chosen riders can gallop down the Via del Duomo and try to capture the star. A small silver star is the prize awarded to those riders who "pierce" the coveted star. At the end of the star contest is the race of the *pariglie*, which starts at the parvis of the church of San Sebastiano where groups of three horses in close side-by-side formation run at full gallop with riders performing spectacular and breathtaking stunts meticulously prepared in the months preceding the *Sartiglia*. At the end of this event, silence falls and the *Componidori* rides back to the place where he was robed and there he finally dismounts. The disrobing ritual starts amidst applause, cheers and drum rolls. The contest is over, the games have come to an end and the horses are back in the stables, but the day is not over yet. Now it is time to celebrate, and it will be a long night.

158-159 *"RUNNING AT THE RINGS" IS A COMPETITION OF SKILL WHERE RIDERS ATTEMPT TO SLIP A LANCE INTO A RING OR STRIKE A TARGET, IN THIS CASE A STAR.*

160 *THE RIDERS HAVE TO INSERT THEIR SWORDS OR THE WOODEN LANCE THROUGH THE HOLE IN THE CENTER OF A TIN STAR, A SYMBOL OF THE EARTH, HANGING FROM A GREEN RIBBON UNDER THE BELL TOWER OF THE CATHEDRAL.*

161 *A TOTAL OF 120 PARTICIPANTS, DIVIDED INTO 40 TEAMS OF THREE RIDERS EACH, TAKE PART IN THE SARTIGLIA. THE ENTIRE CITY OF ORISTANO STOPS AS SPECTATORS THRONG THE STREETS TO WATCH THE HORSES AND RIDERS ALL DECKED OUT WITH COLORFUL AND GLITTERING COSTUMES.*

The last wild horses

ITALY ■ GIARA

THE GIARA HORSE IS ONE OF THE FEW HORSES IN THE WORLD THAT STILL LIVES IN THE WILD.

It thrives, free and proud, in Sardinia and is one of the few breeds of horses that, to some extent, can still be considered to be wild. The Giara Horse, a small and ancient Sardinian steed, has even been defined as a living fossil because its origins date so far back. It would appear that these horses were brought to the island by the Phoenicians and the Greeks in the 5th century. The Giara Horse or Giarino, as it is also called, owes its name to the basalt plateau of volcanic origin where it has always lived in the wild, perfectly integrated with the environment with which it has been indissolubly linked for centuries.

The Giara, or *sa Jara* in the Sardinian language that is spoken in the region, is located in southwestern Sardinia and covers about 45 square kilometers at an altitude varying between 500 and 600 meters above sea level, forming part of the municipalities of Gesturi Tuili, Genoni and Setzu and the provinces of Cagliari, Nuoro and Oristano. The term Giara was coined by local inhabitants precisely because of the harshness of the place; it is rocky and covered with dense vegetation and maquis shrubland. Furthermore, since prehistoric times there has always been very little human settlement on the steep sides of the plateau, thus giving rise to a sort of island within the island. And it was precisely this isolation that has made the Giara Horse so special. The hostile and unspoiled environment, the poor pastures, as well as very little contact with man and other equine populations, have indeed contributed to the process of

selection over time that has produced hardy, tough and spirited animals, with a proud and indomitable character, and that are, above all, of a small size that currently does not exceed a height of 135 cm (13.3 hands) at the withers. Despite its size, it is incorrect to refer to the Giara Horse as a pony. Its reduced morphology, compared to that of traditional horses, is indeed different from that of a small sturdy pony. This is a proper horse which, even today, still presents the essential features described by the earliest enthusiasts who studied Giara Horses over the past centuries. The way of life of Giara Horses is of particular interest in that they have maintained ancestral hierarchies that are typical of wild horses. Indeed, they live in herds made up of a stallion and several adult mares, followed by their respective colts born within the year, and by younger mares and young stallions. The habitat of the Giara Horse has indeed proved to be ideal for the revival, albeit partial, of the typical genotype of the wild horse, a very rare characteristic to find in equine heritage anywhere in the world. A legacy of this involutive evolution of the Giara Horse is its high-spirited, almost untamed character concealed by a calm appearance. Whenever they feel threatened, these horses are capable of unleashing unexpected strength and resistance and fighting courageously. For this reason, to capture the "Giarini" for whatever reason, to identify them or to examine or treat them for medical reasons, is far from an easy undertaking. Once tamed, however, they are much easier to handle and it is not uncommon for these small horses, despite their animosity, to be ridden in competitions by young riders.

162-163 *THE GIARA HORSE IS FAMOUS FOR ITS VIBRANT AND REBELLIOUS NATURE, THE RESULT OF CENTURIES OF SURVIVAL IN THE ISOLATED AND SOMEWHAT HOSTILE ENVIRONMENT OF THE GIARA PLATEAU, WHICH GIVES THE HORSE ITS NAME.*

163 *THE GIARINO LIVES IN HERDS IN ABSOLUTE FREEDOM. IT WAS THIS ENVIRONMENT, WITH ITS NATURAL CYCLES, THAT DETERMINED THE SURVIVAL OF THIS BREED, ONE OF THE FEW THAT CAN STILL BE CALLED WILD.*

ITALY

GIARA

164-165 *Even if it is called the "Giara Pony," its morphology is in fact that of a horse, albeit very small; individuals do not exceed 135 cm at the withers.*

165 *After centuries of living in the wild, Giara horses have integrated perfectly with the habitat of the plateau. The lack of contact with other breeds has also kept them identical to the little horses that were studied and described by early scholars.*

Brilliant Black

ITALY ▪ MURGE

THIS PROUD AND POWERFUL HORSE WITH A JET BLACK COAT WAS ONCE A RELIABLE WORKING PARTNER IN THE COUNTRY, BUT NOW IT IS A GREAT HORSE FOR PLEASURE RIDING.

For centuries, Apulia was not only one of the most beautiful regions of Italy, but also one of the more productive areas for horse breeding. Indeed, this is the homeland of the fine horse of the Murge. Among all the ancient and unique breeds in the south of Italy, the so-called Murgese is the only one to have survived extinction. The Murge is an area that is characterized by woodlands and wood pasture; it includes the towns of Alberobello, Ceglie, Cisternino, Martina Franca, Locorotondo and Noci. These towns are also renowned for breeding donkeys, among which we find the well-known Martina Franca donkey.

The Murgese boasts noble origins, considering that

in ancient times it was bred almost exclusively by the aristocracy. Since 1482, the feudal lords of Apulia, the Acquavivas, Counts of Conversano, and the Caracciolos, Dukes of Martina Franca, would show off these magnificent horses with their brilliant black coats, the result of intelligent crossbreeding of local mares with Andalusian, Oriental, African, Barb and Arab stallions. Indeed, it was the Count of Conversano who imported stallions from Spain and Arabia to produce a new sizable, resistant and strong horse to be used in agriculture. One of the characteristics of the Murgese is indeed its resistance, an asset that derives from the fact that it is bred in a harsh environment that spans 14,000 acres of oak and holm oak woodland. The rather sparse and bushy pastures that develop over the gentle slopes, along with the low rainfall, characterize their habitat. It consists of rugged and arid limestone hills, dotted with white farmhouses, an environment that has contributed to forge the black coat of the Murgese.

But above all, docility and courage characterize the Murgese, which today is deployed in a wide variety of ways, such as light draft work, equestrian tourism and pleasure riding in the country, but also in riding schools, dressage and show jumping as well as hippotherapy.

The Murgese's vigor, its balance, its sure-footedness on all terrains and its great resistance can guarantee safe, long-distance trekking and country rides even for inexperienced riders. The Forestry Corps, who occasionally use the Murgese horses for their work in the open countryside, are well aware of this, as are the many enthusiasts who have been lucky enough to ride these powerful dark bay Italian horses. Apulia is a region that is well worth a visit, and it has many agritourism farms that offer pleasure riding on beautiful Murgeses.

ITALY

MURGE

166 *The Murge plateau, in Apulia, is the home of the Murgese horse, which bears its name. Today this breed is widespread throughout Italy. Thanks to its docility and strength, it is perfect for trekking and pleasure riding.*

166-167 *The charm of the Murgese is unparalleled. Its jet black coat, haughty bearing and the harmony of its gaits make this ancient breed the pride of Italian breeders.*

SLOVENIA

LIPICA

White elegance

SLOVENIA ■ LIPICA

THE FAMOUS LIPIZZANER WHITE HORSES ARE THE STARS OF "HIGH SCHOOL" EQUESTRIANISM.

Lipizzaner horses, with their elegant movements and white coats, are fascinating. For the past four centuries, they have been the undisputed stars of the famous Spanish Riding School of Vienna, founded in 1572. Through their daily exercises, they have witnessed a glorious but very troubled history. The Lipizzaner breed, founded in 1580 by the Archduke Charles of Styria, the third son of the Habsburg Emperor Ferdinand I, is one of the oldest in Europe. The name comes from Lipizza, the Italian name of what is now the Slovenian town of Lipica. This is where the Archduke Charles chose to found a stud farm for breeding horses destined for the Court of Vienna. The breed was founded starting with Italian mares from the Italian provinces of Aquileia, Polesine and Verona, and later Danish females and Andalusian, Neapolitan and then Arab stallions and mares. It is from these origins that the typical white coat derives; this characteristic was intentionally selected by the Imperial House of Austria right from the start.

The horse as it is known today reached its definitive conformation in the middle of the 18th century, during the reign of Maria Theresa of Austria, when her husband, Francis of Lorraine, took a great interest in developing the royal stud farm. The result was a compact horse with sturdy limbs and powerful movements, a graceful horse with a particularly noble and typically "baroque" bearing – essentially all the characteristics that were in demand at the time. Since then, the Lipizzaner has had to withstand many hardships, including natural and historical disasters and war. The breed, however, has escaped unscathed from dismemberment, divisions, epidemics, fires, earthquakes, wars and the division of the spoils of what was once the territory of the Austro-Hungarian Empire, and succeeded in handing down to our days its ancient history.

The last of these vicissitudes is perhaps the most outstanding and dates back to the end of World War II when the Lipizzaners, previously requisitioned by the Germans, were near Prague, in the territory assigned to the Soviets. To save the breed, in April 1945 the famous American General George Patton decided to move the Lipizzaners to Montenegro, an area under the control of the United States, before the advancing Soviet armed forces reached them. This interest in Lipizzaner horses also convinced the Austrian Colonel Alois Podhajsky, who had won the bronze medal for individual dressage at the Berlin Olympics of 1936 and was director of the Spanish Riding School of Vienna during the war, to apply for Patton's protection to safeguard the fine stallions of the school that he had moved from Vienna, which was

168-169 *THIS LIPIZZANER STALLION GALLOPING FREELY SHOWS OFF ALL THE ENERGY AND ELEGANCE OF ITS BREED. TODAY THERE ARE 6 MALE AND 15 FEMALE BLOODLINES. THESE ARE THE "CLASSICAL" BLOODLINES FROM WHICH ALL LIPIZZANERS BORN TODAY ARE DERIVED.*

168 *THE LIPIZZANER HORSE-BREEDING FARM WAS FOUNDED IN 1580 IN LIPIZZA (LIPICA), WHICH IS NOW IN SLOVENIA. FOALS OF THIS BREED, WHICH IS THE OLDEST HORSE BREED IN EUROPE, ARE STILL BORN HERE TODAY.*

subjected to heavy bombing. The Americans thus divided the Lipizzaners into three groups and assigned them to Austria, Yugoslavia and Italy together with their Stud Books. This invaluable documentation starts with records of those born in 1810, but it has also been possible to trace the ancestors of many of the horses born two centuries ago. The "oldest" of these was a mare named Colomba (Dove) born in 1738. The Stud Books document the antiquity of this horse even through the bloodlines that are still active. These are the "classical" bloodlines from which all Lipizzaners born today are derived: six male lines and 15 female lines. Ever since the breed was founded, Lipizzaners have always been purebreds, developed to maintain the characteristics of a "baroque horse" with the outstanding qualities of a "riding school" horse essential for parade, dressage and Classical High School equestrianism. Due to its extraordinary gift of learning, together with its will, obedience, strength and endurance, the Lipizzaner is perfect for all uses, especially for light combined driving and countryside leisure riding.

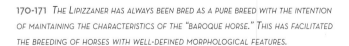

170-171 THE LIPIZZANER HAS ALWAYS BEEN BRED AS A PURE BREED WITH THE INTENTION OF MAINTAINING THE CHARACTERISTICS OF THE "BAROQUE HORSE." THIS HAS FACILITATED THE BREEDING OF HORSES WITH WELL-DEFINED MORPHOLOGICAL FEATURES.

172-173 IN ADDITION TO THEIR UNDISPUTED QUALITIES, LIPIZZANER HORSES ARE FAMOUS FOR THEIR TYPICAL COLOR. LIKE ALL GRAY HORSES, THEY ARE NOT BORN WITH THIS COAT, WHICH ACQUIRES ITS COLOR OVER TIME.

AUSTRIA

VIENNA

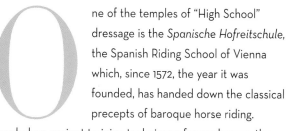

Baroque horse riding

AUSTRIA ■ VIENNA

FOR CENTURIES, THE SPANISH RIDING SCHOOL OF VIENNA
HAS MAINTAINED A GREAT EQUESTRIAN TRADITION.

One of the temples of "High School" dressage is the *Spanische Hofreitschule*, the Spanish Riding School of Vienna which, since 1572, the year it was founded, has handed down the classical precepts of baroque horse riding. Founded on ancient training techniques for warhorses, the *Hohe Schule* (High School or *Haute Ecole*) is based on a horse's natural movements, highlighted in their purest form and with the utmost perfection. The Spanish Riding School of Vienna is the oldest institution in the equestrian world: it was founded by the Habsburgs to teach the nobility the "art of horse riding" at a time when all manner of celebrations, parades and processions were important occasions for the image of the royal court of the Austro-Hungarian Empire. It owes its name to the Spanish horses that were used originally; they have now been replaced by the Lipizzaner horses, a prized breed that has inextricably linked its destiny with that of the Viennese school.

Today, the school is the pride of Austria and is kept alive as a vital cultural and historical institution of immense touristic importance. Indeed, the daily training sessions, and the performances that are held twice a week in the "Winter Riding School" in the Imperial Hofburg Palace, are open to the public. The Winter Riding School was inaugurated in 1735, and since then it has been the venue where the school riders, with their gray Lipizzaner stallions, stage their "High School" performance. The Spanish Riding School of Vienna uses only Lipizzaner stallions that are bred in Piber, a town not far from Vienna. They are trained by the riders of the school following a long, gradual and, as much as possible, natural work schedule that starts when the stallions are 4 years old. Even the riders are selected very carefully. It takes no less than seven or eight years to train a rider up to standard to be authorized to train a young stallion for "High School" exercises.

These exercises are called the "Airs Above the Ground." In some "airs" the horse's limbs do not rise high above the ground, as in the *piaffe*, a collected trot carried out on the spot, or the *pirouette*, a full rotation of the shoulders of the horse around the hind inside leg. There are those "airs" in which the horse raises two limbs off the ground: the *passage*, a slow trot in which the forelegs are raised, and the *levade*, in which the horse lifts its front legs and lowers its hindquarters with all its weight on its bent hind legs. And then there are the most spectacular and difficult "airs" in which all the horse's limbs rise from the ground, as in the *courbette*, defined as an extension of the *levade*, as the horse comes off the ground with its hind legs and leaps forward. A further extension of this movement, coupled with a vigorous backward kick of the hind legs while the body of the horse is completely suspended in mid-air for a few moments, is called the *capriole*. It takes at least six years' work to train a stallion to perform in public in a *Schulquadrille*, and only a very few, the most talented and sensitive ones, can perform the most spectacular "airs."

174-175 *ATTENDING THE SCHULQUADRILLE, THE EXHIBITION OF HORSES AND RIDERS OF THE SPANISCHE HOFREITSCHULE (SPANISH SCHOOL) IN VIENNA'S HOFBURG WINTER RIDING SCHOOL, IS LIKE RELIVING THE AUSTERE ATMOSPHERE OF THE HABSBURG COURT.*

174 *IN THE WINTER RIDING SCHOOL IN THE BEAUTIFUL HALL THAT WAS ONCE USED FOR COURT BANQUETS, THE HORSEMEN TRAIN THE MAGNIFICENT LIPIZZANERS IN THE FINEST EQUESTRIAN ARTS.*

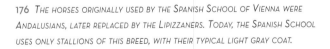

176 THE HORSES ORIGINALLY USED BY THE SPANISH SCHOOL OF VIENNA WERE
ANDALUSIANS, LATER REPLACED BY THE LIPIZZANERS. TODAY, THE SPANISH SCHOOL
USES ONLY STALLIONS OF THIS BREED, WITH THEIR TYPICAL LIGHT GRAY COAT.

176-177 ALL THE HORSES USED IN "HIGH SCHOOL" PERFORMANCES ARE TRAINED BY
THE HORSEMEN OF THE SPANISH SCHOOL. MANY YEARS OF TRAINING ARE NECESSARY
FOR A RIDER TO REACH THIS LEVEL.

178-179 *THE PUBLIC CAN WATCH THE DAILY WORK OF THE LIPIZZANER STALLIONS DURING TRAINING. THE OFFICIAL PERFORMANCES, INCLUDING ALL THE SPECTACULAR HIGH SCHOOL ROUTINES, ARE HELD TWICE A WEEK.*

In the land of the Csikos

HUNGARY ■ PUSZTA

THE GREAT EXPANSES OF THE *PUSZTA* ARE THE CRADLE OF THE FINE BREEDS REARED BY THE CSIKOS, THE HUNGARIAN COWBOYS.

Hungary is renowned as the homeland of horses par excellence. Indeed, the horses of the Hungarian *puszta* belong to fine breeds but, as often happens, they owe much of their fame to the men who, over time, have raised and trained them, establishing an indissoluble link with them. And this is why talking about Hungarian horses means talking about the Csikos, the famous herdsmen and skilled horsemen. If breeds such as the Gidran, Nonius and Furioso-North Star are known and appreciated all over the world, it is thanks to the Csikos who, dressed in their traditional costumes, are still active as horse breeders and trainers. The Csikos, like their mounts, are famous everywhere, above all for their exceptional horsemanship and for the skill and courage they display in equestrian shows and acrobatic exercises. The best-known of their routines is the "*Puszta* Five," in which a rider leads five galloping horses with long reins, standing on the backs of two of them.

In Hungary, men and horses are one, but one other thing the various breeds of Hungarian horses have in common is their ancestor, the Arabian horse. In 1526 Hungary fell under Turkish domination. Since then, there have always been a significant number of Oriental horses in these lands, and these would influence indelibly the horses reared in the *puszta*. Subsequently, state farms such as those of Mezöhegyes (founded in 1785) and Bábolna (founded in 1769) went down in history for developing Hungarian breeds to the levels of prestige for which they have come to be famous. Both farms produced brilliant horses for the cavalry and to tow artillery until 1816, when the strategy changed to favor horses that were more markedly Arabian. And in Mezöhegyes this is what gave rise to the Gidran,

also known as the "Anglo-Arab of Hungary," a breed that is famous for its characteristic chestnut coat and for its exceptional fiery temperament, courage and strength.

Mezöhegyes, however, was not only the cradle of the Gidran. In 1813 the Hussars returned home with a light bay stallion captured from the French at Leipzig. He was called Nonius Senior and was used as a breeding stud in Mezöhegyes. Despite his less than exceptional morphology, Nonius Senior proved to be successful for breeding purposes when crossed with Neapolitan and Andalusian mares, and his male offspring, crossed with Arab and Kladruber mares, established the characteristics of the Nonius breed. Bay and black, resistant, strong, sensitive, docile and versatile, the Nonius is excellent as a light draft horse and fares well as a riding horse, and it is superlative for harness racing.

Another notable Hungarian breed is the Furioso-North Star. Even in this case, the name is derived from the founding sire, or rather the two recognized founding sires in this case. Its origins date back to the Austro-Hungarian Empire. In 1841 a Thoroughbred stallion named Furioso was imported to Mezöhegyes and subsequently in 1844 a Norfolk Roadster (an English half-breed driving horse) called North Star was also brought to the breeding farm. When crossed with the female descendants of Nonius Senior, these stallions produced excellent results, generating fine colts that were originally kept separate. In 1885 however, the two lines were merged and the resulting breed of elegant, graceful and well-made horses assumed the name of Furioso-North Star, a breed that specialized above all as a driving horse, even at a competitive level, spreading widely thanks to its temperament and the fact that it is also a worthy riding horse.

180-181 *THE CSIKOS, THE COWBOYS OF THE PUSZTA, ARE EXCELLENT RIDERS AND TRAINERS. THEY HAVE CONTRIBUTED TO THE SELECTION AND DEVELOPMENT OF THE FINE BREEDS OF HORSES BRED IN HUNGARY.*

181 *THERE IS A REAL SYMBIOSIS BETWEEN MAN AND HORSES IN THE WORLD OF THE CSIKOS. THE ABILITY OF THESE RIDERS IN DEALING WITH THEIR ANIMALS, ALONG WITH THE RESPECT THE HORSES HAVE FOR MAN, MAKE THEIR RELATIONSHIP UNIQUE IN THE WHOLE WORLD.*

182-183 *THE "PUSZTA FIVE" IS ONE OF THE EQUESTRIAN EXERCISES TYPICAL OF THE CSIKOS, WHO ARE FAMOUS FOR THEIR ACROBATIC SKILL.*

HUNGARY

PUSZTA

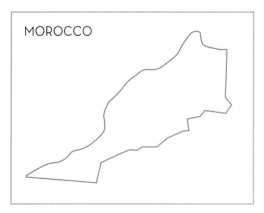

MOROCCO

A distinguished leader

MOROCCO

FROM ANTIQUITY TO MODERN TIMES, THE BARB HAS ALWAYS HAD A MAJOR ROLE IN HISTORY, MOVING FROM ONE CONTINENT TO ANOTHER.

The Barb is not a well-known horse breed. Nevertheless, it has earned its place in history over the centuries, not only for the beauty and elegance of its features and movements, but above all because of its generous heart. These horses, by nature, do not hesitate to "go beyond their call of duty" and run the extra mile.

Their history is closely linked to the population that has bred them for centuries. The term "Barb" is derived from "barbarian," an inhabitant of the Barbary Coast: in other words, of the Maghreb, or Northwest Africa (Morocco, Algeria, Tunisia and the western part of Libya, better known as Tripolitania).

The Barb has been involved in many important historical events thanks to its temperament and courage. Originally from Algeria, the Barb played a part in the achievements of the Byzantines as early as the 6th century A.D. In the 7th century, Tarik Ben Ziad arrived in Spain with a cavalry of 7,000 Barb horses. From Spain the Barb reached France, accompanying the long march of Islam through Europe. In later times, it was always appreciated in Arab cavalries. Indeed, it was with Barbs that Arab cavalries set out to conquer Sicily and Apulia.

The origins of the Neapolitan and Murgese horses, two of the oldest and most appreciated Italian breeds, are to be found in the Barb horse. And it is again in the Barb that Spanish horses find their origins, thanks to the presence in Cordoba of one of the most important Barb stud farms. The Barb spread rapidly to France and England, where it played an important role in many major historical events. Because of its widespread presence in European countries with the most important horse breeding traditions, many of the best-known breeds have some Barb blood.

Today most Barb horses are in North Africa, above all in Algeria, where there are about 10,000 of them and another 90,000 Arab-Barbs (Barbs crossed with Arab thoroughbreds). The Barb is approximately 1.57 meters high at the withers and today, in Algeria, it is the undisputed winner of endurance races thanks to its sturdy constitution. However, it also excels in show jumping competitions and dressage events. Its performance in races organized by the Algerian "Societe des Courses" (Horse Racing Authority), over distances of 1,800 to 2,400 meters and in dressage events, is renowned.

The Barb also has a well-defined role in Algerian "fantasy" shows. Horses set off at full gallop over a distance of 500 meters, to be stopped at the same time. All of this is done while the riders shoot with their rifles. The number of horses running together varies and can be up to 17, all side-by-side.

Traditionally, three varieties of Barbs exist in Algeria, coming from three different territories with different characteristics. There is a highland species that is more slender and elegant, an Eastern variety that is larger and sturdier, and the Barb of the plains and the coast, which is smaller and more compact.

184-185 THIS BEAUTIFUL BARB'S DAPPLE-GRAY COAT INDICATES THAT IT IS A YOUNG HORSE. THE GRAY COLOR TENDS TO FADE OVER THE YEARS UNTIL IT BECOMES ALMOST WHITE.

184 THIS HORSE'S HOMELAND IS NORTH AFRICA, THE LAND WHERE ITS BREED GREW AND SPREAD TO BECOME THE INDISPENSABLE COMPANION OF THE PEOPLE.

186-187 THE BARB MOVES WITH AGILITY ON SAND. IT IS TIRELESS AND SURE OF ITSELF AND WAS A PROTAGONIST IN THE BYZANTINE WORLD AS EARLY AS THE 6TH CENTURY A.D.

188-189 *In addition to pure Barb horses, today in North Africa there are many horses that are the product of crossbreeding between Arabian and Barb horses, including the Arabian-Barb breed.*

189 *Thanks to its physical endurance and its structure, the Barb is able to withstand the arid desert climate and is the undisputed champion in endurance trials.*

190-191 *The breathtaking scenery in the cities that rise from the desert, and the contrast of colors between the horsemen's garments and the horses' decorations, render these pictures particularly evocative and thrilling.*

191 *The Barb is a proud horse with an elegant bearing. Even though it is very fiery and high-spirited, it can be well behaved and quiet and stay on guard for hours.*

192 TOP *A herd of Barb horses set off at a gallop while their riders fire rifles into the air: this is one of the most thrilling moments of the "fantasy" shows organized in Algeria.*

192 BOTTOM *Another moment from a "fantasy" performance: the horses are still, lined up and ready to set off. Their pricked up ears turned forward, indicating that they are on the alert for their riders' commands.*

192-193 *In this evocative picture of a group of Barb horses with gray coats, adorned with splendid rich trappings, the horsemen's traditional festive costumes are also worthy of note.*

The purest of the pure

EGYPT

THE ARAB OR ARABIAN HORSE IS THE MOST IMPORTANT
PUREBRED HORSE IN THE WORLD, BUT IT IS ONLY
THE EGYPTIAN ARAB THAT CAN CLAIM THE "ASIL" NAME.

It is the most beautiful, the proudest and the most elegant horse. And it is the purest of horses. The Arabian horse, or rather the purebred Arabian, is bred the world over, but its birthplace is the Arabian Peninsula. The "Asil" name, however, which refers to those individuals that descend exclusively from the horses of the desert, is now reserved only for Egyptian Arabians. The origins of the Arabian horse are lost in the mists of time, somewhere between history and legend intertwined with Islamic culture and the culture of Bedouin tribes. And indeed, it is thanks to them that the purity of the breed has been passed down, in its full splendor, to this very day.

The Bedouins have always considered the horse a divine gift. After all, it was the Prophet Muhammad himself who made it almost a religious duty to breed Asil horses. In his precepts, Muhammad established that in order to ensure the purity of the breed, only "noble" mares, meaning mares that had mated only with Asil stallions, could bear Asil Horses. Horses that were born outside the scope of such crossbreeding requirements were still considered Arabian horses, but they were called "Kadish," that is, impure. Originally, all "pure" Arabian horses were called Asil horses, indicating that they belonged to one of the five most prestigious families descending from the five mares that, according to legend, were chosen by Muhammad, but the ancestors of today's horses indicate that only the Egyptian Arabian, the so-called "straight Egyptian," can be considered an "Asil," meaning "a pure horse of the desert."

The need for such a distinction was determined by the wide distribution of the breed as a result of the expansion of the Moors into Europe. Thanks to its charm, its power and all of its other outstanding qualities, the Arabian horse was coveted by the nobility and the armies of all countries, both as a gift and as spoils of war. It was so much appreciated that between the 18th and 19th centuries, the first state-owned farms made an appearance in the Old World, continuously importing stallions and mares from the Arabian Peninsula. The prized Arabian horses of European breeding farms like Marbach in Germany, Bábolna in Hungary, Janow Podlaski in Poland, and also Tarbes, Pau and Pompadour in France and the famous English farm of the Blunt family – where the famous Crabbet Arabian originated at the end of the 19th century – contributed significantly to the exceptional development of the breed in the world, although individual horses from these farms are not always of exclusive Asil ancestry.

The turning point for the recognition of the "Straight Egyptian" came shortly after the Second World War, when in 1949, Tibor von Pettkoe-Szandtner, former head of the Bábolna breeding farm, took over El Zahraa, the Egyptian state breeding farm. Based on a rigorous assessment of the Asil origins of mating couples and by assessing the morphology and gait of each individual, in only six years, von Pettkoe-Szandtner succeeded in implementing fundamental selective breeding. This task was facilitated by Nazeer, the most important Asil stallion of all time that the Hungarian general had the merit of discovering on a remote Egyptian stud farm. Nazeer and his descendants are responsible for the diffusion, around the whole world, of the Egyptian Arabian Asils, the true horses of the desert.

EGYPT

194 THE PUREBRED ARABIAN (PBA) IS A HORSE THAT HAS BEEN BRED IN PURITY FOR
OVER A MILLENNIUM AND IS THE ONLY ONE TO HAVE HAD A SIGNIFICANT INFLUENCE
ON THE EMERGENCE AND IMPROVEMENT OF ALMOST ALL OTHER KNOWN BREEDS.

195 TRADITION HAS IT THAT MUHAMMAD IS RESPONSIBLE FOR THE PURITY OF
THE ASILS. INDEED, IN HIS PRECEPTS THE PROPHET LAID DOWN THE RULES THAT
THE DESERT TRIBES HAVE APPLIED SINCE, GENERATION AFTER GENERATION.

196-197 FOR SOME TIME NOW, THE PUREBRED ARABIAN HORSE HAS BECOME
AN INTERNATIONAL HORSE THAT IS BRED THE WORLD OVER. OF ALL THE EXISTING
BLOOD LINES, IT IS ONLY THE ONE TO WHICH THE EGYPTIAN ARABIANS BELONG
THAT IS CONSIDERED TO BE ASIL.

197 DESPITE CENTURIES OF ISLAMIC HISTORY AND CULTURE, THE ASIL OWES
MUCH TO A EUROPEAN, TIBOR VON PETTKOE-SZANDTNER, FORMER DIRECTOR OF
THE BÁBOLNA HORSE BREEDING FARM WHO SINCE 1949 HAS MANAGED EL ZAHRAAT,
THE EGYPTIAN STATE HORSE BREEDING FARM.

NIGERIA

KATSINA

The Durbar Festival

NIGERIA ▪ KATSINA

IN MANY CITIES IN NIGERIA THE FESTIVAL OF DURBAR
IS CELEBRATED ANNUALLY. SOME OF THESE CELEBRATIONS
ARE MAJOR TOURIST ATTRACTIONS.

Nigeria is the most densely populated nation in West Africa. This land is often the scene of picturesque and entertaining local festivals that have ancient traditions and are varied in nature. Festivals are organized to celebrate events as diverse as the harvest, betrothals, the appointment of a new tribal chief, religious festivals and celebrations, and even funerals. Every occasion is a good excuse to dance and dress up. In ancient times, the protagonists of the dances were members of various tribes themselves, but today troupes of professional dancers move from village to village taking part in each of these festivals, some of which have become true tourist attractions.

The most famous event is the Durbar Festival, held in various cities of Nigeria during the major Islamic festivities of Eid al-Fitr and Eid al-Adha, which mark the end of the month of Ramadan. This annual festival is one of the oldest, dating back several centuries to a time when the northern states were still using horses in battle. Every city, district, and noble family had to contribute to the defense of the Emirate by forming its own regiment. Once or twice a year, the military chiefs of the Emirate invited the various regiments for a military parade, called Durbar, in honor of the Emir and his most important dignitaries, during which the regiments had to demonstrate their loyalty, their military training and all their equestrian skills. Today, Durbar festivals are celebrated to honor heads of state.

Of all the modern Durbar Festivals, the most spectacular is probably the one that takes place in the city of Katsina. The show begins with a recitation of prayers, followed by a procession of horsemen in the public square in front of the residence of the Emir. He is the last to appear, along with his entourage, to be honored by his subjects.

Riders cross the square at full gallop in groups passing just a few feet away from the Emir with their shining swords drawn. Then they stop abruptly right in front of him for the ritual salute, raising the tips of their swords high into the sky. Closing the parade are the proud Dogari, the regimental guards. At the end of this ritual, the Emir and his guards withdraw and the festivities begin. Brass bands and the beat of the drums accompany the traditional singing and dancing.

198-199 *DURBAR IS A TRADITIONAL EQUESTRIAN FESTIVAL THAT IS ORGANIZED IN SEVERAL CITIES IN NIGERIA DURING THE MUSLIM CELEBRATIONS OF EID AL-FITR AND EID AL-ADHA. GROUPS OF RIDERS FROM NEARBY VILLAGES COME ON HORSEBACK TO PAY HOMAGE TO THE EMIR.*

198 *THE ORIGINS OF THE FESTIVAL DATE BACK TO THE DAYS WHEN HORSES WERE USED IN BATTLE. IN AFRICAN TERRITORY, IN GENERAL, THERE IS A PREFERENCE FOR BARB HORSES OR ARABIAN-BARB CROSSBREEDS AS THEY ARE VERY RESISTANT TO DESERT CLIMATES, THANKS TO THEIR PHYSICAL STRUCTURE THAT MAKES THEM PARTICULARLY AGILE.*

199 *HORSEMEN IN TRADITIONAL ATTIRE WITH COLORFUL TURBANS, TYPICAL OF THE LOCAL TRIBES, PARADE THROUGH THE STREETS OF KANO DURING THE FESTIVAL.*

200-201 *THE COLORFUL COSTUMES WORN BY MEMBERS OF DIFFERENT TRIBES AND THE ORIGINAL ORNAMENTAL HORSE TRAPPINGS CREATE AN EXTRAORDINARY ATMOSPHERE FOR FOREIGN VISITORS.*

The wildest in the world

MONGOLIA ■ HUSTAI NATIONAL PARK

THE MONGOLIAN HORSE, *EQUUS PRZEWALSKII*, IS PROBABLY THE ONLY TRUE WILD HORSE ALIVE TODAY.

For many of us, the image of the horse is still that of a wild animal galloping free in wild open expanses, over endless unspoiled lands. Reality, however, is quite different. The only true wild horse that is still alive today is the *Equus Przewalskii*, a native of Mongolia. It disappeared from its natural habitat several decades ago and it lives in large natural parks. In recent years, however, an expensive project coordinated by ethologists has been launched for the reintroduction and re-population of the Przewalski in its natural environment.

Mongolia is certainly not an easy or hospitable region. Indeed, in its boundless steppes the temperature in winter can fall to as low as 40 or 50 degrees below zero, and winter lasts from October to May. The Przewalski horse, however, is strong and resilient, and it succeeded in re-adapting to the harsh rigors of its land of origin rather quickly. Today, these horses live in herds, mainly in southwestern Mongolia in the Hustai National Park, which was declared a specially protected area in 1993 and made available, by the government, for the reintroduction

and repopulation project of this breed that is a symbol of Mongolia.

The Przewalski horse is an exceptionally wild creature, and indeed it is one of the wildest animal species in the world. Because of its small size – it is only 124 to 144 cm (12.2-14.2 hands) high at the withers – it is often considered more of a pony than a horse.

The Przewalski's coat makes it very special and unusual; its ears have a frame of black hairs just inside the edge, its nostrils and lips are dark gray, its body is usually honey-colored, ranging from lighter to darker shades, becoming darker and thicker during the extremely cold winter. Its mane is short and bristly like a zebra's – an animal with which it shares other characteristics – and black like its tail and lower limbs.

The Przewalski horse is a wild animal and as such it must live in total freedom. Indeed, Przewalski horses in captivity become aggressive because they fear the presence of man for the simple reason that they are not used to him and therefore consider him to be a potential predator. The Przewalski horse today is entrusted to the care of the Foundation for the Preservation and Protection of the Przewalski Horse (FPPPH).

202-203 *The Przewalski's sturdy and resistant constitution has allowed it to survive in the difficult territory of Mongolia, where temperatures in winter drop well below zero.*

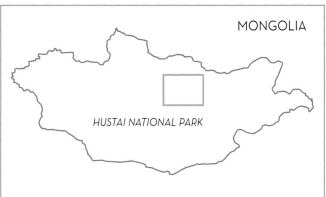

MONGOLIA

HUSTAI NATIONAL PARK

204 *Stocky and small in stature, with a height ranging from 124 to 144 cm at the withers, the Przewalski is considered more of a pony than a horse.*

205 *The Przewalski has a honey-colored coat and a short coarse black mane. Even its lower legs and its tail are black, likewise the hair that frames its ears. Its lips and nostrils are dark gray.*

206-207 *Being wild animals, these equines live in herds in total freedom. They have been declared a protected species, and today they live in the Hustai National Park that was allocated to them by the Government of Mongolia.*

The Litang Horse Festival

PEOPLE'S REPUBLIC OF CHINA ■ LITANG

THE SETTING IS WONDERFUL WESTERN SICHUAN, OFFERING A UNIQUE OPPORTUNITY TO BECOME ACQUAINTED WITH THE HABITS AND CUSTOMS OF THE TIBETANS AND THEIR HORSES.

The Tibetan plateau, to the north of the Himalayas, is the highest region of the planet, with an average altitude of over 4,500 meters. Unsurprisingly, it is also called the "Roof of the World." The land is rich in history and mysticism as well as breathtaking natural scenery, and it is visited each year by a large number of tourists from all over the world. The Tibet Autonomous Region, which belongs to the People's Republic of China, covers a significant portion of this plateau, which slopes downward to the east toward western Sichuan, an area that was historically part of "Greater Tibet" and remains within the area of Tibetan cultural influence (as do some regions in other provinces in western and southwestern China, such as Qinghai, Gansu and Yunnan).

Litang is located in the western part of the province of Sichuan, in the southwestern portion of the Tibetan Autonomous Prefecture of Garzê where almost 80 percent of the population is of Tibetan ethnic origin. Litang is a small town in the region of Kham and, at an altitude of 4,100 meters, it is one of the highest places in the world. Above all, it is one of those magical places, far away from the traditional tourist trails and the more famous and popular destinations, that offers a unique opportunity to enter the real life of local Tibetan people to witness truly exceptional events.

One of these is the Litang Horse Festival, the largest and most evocative among the traditional Tibetan cultural festivals. It is rendered even more spectacular by the magnificent surrounding landscape: peat pastures, carpets of little wild flowers and edelweiss, snow-capped peaks, glaciers and high passes where you can catch a glimpse of tents and nomads, yaks and horses. Fascinating ancient Buddhist monasteries, where traditional ceremonies are celebrated every day, are waiting to be discovered. The festival consists of displays of horsemanship by Khampa horsemen, nomadic warriors dressed in sumptuous costumes, decorated with fine brocades, embroidery and glittering jewels. They take part in wild races, displays of riding skills and a dance that represents the competition between different troops, lined up in their traditional costumes. The Tibetan pony is agile, nimble and courageous, and the undisputed protagonist of this show.

In addition to the events that revolve around horses, which attract the attention of everyone present, there are examples of local arts and crafts and a fair with a display of local products. The festival begins on 1 August and lasts for 10 days, and although it takes place in the summer, it is nonetheless bitterly cold because of the altitude. More than 20,000 Tibetans, including nomads, monks and people from all the neighboring cities, gather here during this period. The horse displays, therefore, become a reason for meeting and an opportunity to give life to religious celebrations.

PEOPLE'S REPUBLIC OF CHINA

LITANG

208-209 THE GROUND IS SCATTERED WITH BRIGHTLY COLORED TENTS PAINTED WITH TRADITIONAL TIBETAN SYMBOLS. THEY SHELTER THE NUMEROUS VISITORS WHO ARE DRAWN HERE EACH YEAR BY THE LITANG HORSE FESTIVAL.

208 LEFT MORE THAN 20,000 TIBETANS GATHER HERE FOR 10 DAYS IN AUGUST FOR THE LITANG FESTIVAL AND THE CEREMONIES THAT TAKE PLACE IN THIS AREA. IN THE PICTURE, IS THE KORLAM, THE CIRCUMAMBULATION AROUND TRAKAR LATHSA, "THE SACRED WHITE STONE ABOVE THE VALLEY".

208 RIGHT THE FESTIVAL IS AN IMPORTANT MEETING FOR ENTHUSIASTS OF EQUESTRIAN DISCIPLINES BUT ALSO A UNIQUE OCCASION TO ADMIRE THE TRADITIONAL LOCAL COSTUMES WITH FLAMBOYANT DECORATIONS, LIKE THE ONES WORN BY THIS GROUP OF WOMEN.

210 *The Khampa, nomadic Tibetan warriors from the region of Kham, are the undisputed protagonists of the event. They display their riding skills wearing sumptuous decorated costumes.*

210-211 *The brightly colored costumes and the typical horse decorations enrich the Litang Festival that is unique in its genre, above all for its atmosphere and the beauty of its location.*

212 OF ALL THE MOUNTS OF THE KHAMPA, THE TIBETAN RACING PONIES ARE PARTICULARLY APPRECIATED. THEY ARE AGILE AND FAST AND MOVE HARMONIOUSLY AS THEIR RIDERS PERFORM THEIR ROUTINES.

212-213 ON THE LITANG PLATEAU AGAINST THE BACKDROP OF THE EXTRAORDINARY LANDSCAPE THAT SURROUNDS THIS EVENT, PARTICIPANTS PUT THEMSELVES TO THE TEST IN ARCHERY AND RIDING COMPETITIONS.

The Horses of Warriors

INDIA ▪ RAJASTHAN

ONCE THE COMPANIONS OF HINDU WARRIORS, TODAY
THEY ARE THE INDISPENSABLE AND IRREPLACEABLE
MOUNTS OF THE INDIAN STATE POLICE.

Rajputana is a historic region in northwestern India. It lies amid windswept rocks and wide expanses of sand. It coincides almost completely with the modern state of Rajasthan and its name is linked to the Rajputs, one of the most important groups in the Hindu warrior caste known as Kshatriyas. It is here, between history and legend, that we find the roots of the Marwari horse, named after the Marwar region, today's Jodhpur region in western Rajasthan. The Marwari horse can live in extreme conditions, in arid and desolate areas, enduring thirst and surviving for quite a while with little or no food. It soon proved to be very gifted for the art of war, thanks to its extraordinary sense of direction and highly developed sense of hearing that enabled it to perceive even the most distant noises. These horses were believed to be divine and superior to men, even those of royal blood, and only members of the warrior caste were allowed to ride them. In battle, the Marwari horse would become one with its rider both in victory and in defeat. Indian literature is full of stories related to these excellent war horses, and there are many tales of wounded soldiers brought home to safety by their horses.

The Marwari is sturdy, compact, elegant and well-proportioned, with particularly long thin limbs. Thanks to its long legs, it can cross the desert, keeping its belly farther from the sand and therefore better protected from the excessive heat. It has small hooves and slightly sloping shoulders, so it can pull its hooves out of the sand with less effort, thus saving energy over long distances. In addition to the three usual gaits, it is endowed with a fourth gait, the so-called *revaal*, which is suitable for long distances as its major characteristic is minimal vertical movement, giving the impression that the horse is gliding over the sand. Its height varies from 150 to 160 cm (14.7 to 15.7 hands) at the withers and it can have any kind of coat.

The breed is distinguished by its ears. Small and mobile, they are turned inward and they often end up touching each other at the tips. It seems that this phenomenon derives from the habit of manipulating the ears of the Marwari from an early age to give them a graceful and regal appearance. Thanks to its elegant bearing, today this horse is successfully used in dressage, while its dexterity and agility render it highly suitable for polo. Its gentle gait, on the other hand, makes the Marwari ideal for trekking over long distances.

For its legendary courage in battle, recounted in the ancient sagas of the exploits of Hindu warriors, and for its qualities of endurance and elegance, the Marwari is used today by the Punjabi police, by the police in the capital city, New Delhi, and by the President's Bodyguard, the elite household cavalry regiment of the Indian army that escorts and protects the President of the Republic of India.

214-215 *THE ESCORT OF THE PRESIDENT OF THE REPUBLIC OF INDIA IS PREPARING FOR THE CEREMONY OF THE CHANGING OF THE GUARD AGAINST THE BACKDROP OF RASHTRAPATI BHAVAN, THE PRESIDENTIAL PALACE IN NEW DELHI.*

215 *DURING THE CEREMONY, THE PRESIDENT'S BODYGUARD MARCHES IN FORMATION FOR 40 MINUTES ALONG THE RAJPATH BOULEVARD, FROM THE RASHTRAPATI BHAVAN TO THE MINISTRY OF DEFENSE AND BACK.*

RAJASTHAN

INDIA

216 *The distinguishing features of the Marwari are its elegant curved neck and its long head with an aquiline profile and scimitar-shaped ears that are small and turned inward so that they touch at the tips.*

216-217 *In ancient battles on horseback, the Marwari horse showed extraordinary courage and loyalty. Many legends tell of wounded warriors rescued by their steeds.*

218-219 *In the early morning mist, members of the President's Bodyguard regiment train their horses for the complicated maneuvers they will perform during official ceremonies.*

219 *Members of the President's Bodyguard regiment practice complex acrobatic routines. In addition to ceremonial duties, the President's Bodyguard has other responsibilities and, as an elite regiment of the Indian Army, has been present in various theaters of war.*

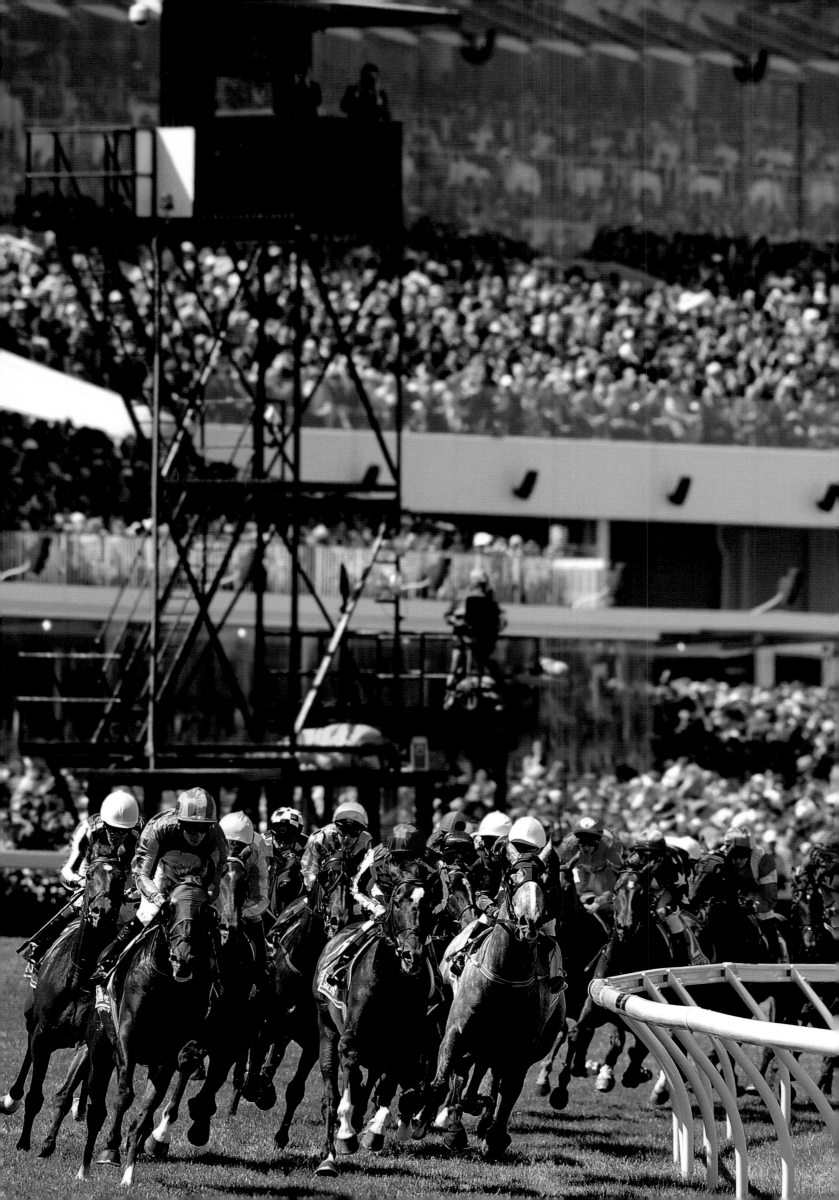

Get ready everybody, it's the Melbourne Cup racing carnival

AUSTRALIA ■ MELBOURNE

EACH YEAR, AUSTRALIANS RENEW THEIR PASSION
FOR THOROUGHBRED HORSE RACING AND BETTING IN THIS
EXCEPTIONAL EVENT THAT IS FULL OF OLD CHARM.

Since 1877, the first Tuesday of November has been a holiday in Melbourne, but it is not the celebration of a historical event or the feast of a saint. The occasion is one of the most famous horse races in the world, the Melbourne Cup. And so on that day, everyone and everything come to a halt, at least for a few minutes, to watch this historic race that has been run since 1861. For the occasion, Flemington Racecourse becomes the scene of a real social event, with areas reserved for members of the most exclusive clubs and with the grandstand and open areas all filled with a very festive crowd. Whoever is not at the racecourse will be glued to the radio or the television to watch the race, stride by stride, as the powerful thoroughbreds brave the 2-mile race to the finishing line, hoping above all to make a betting win. Indeed, in keeping with Anglo-Saxon tradition, everybody bets. The Melbourne Cup Racing Carnival however, is more than just a race. It is a sort of rendezvous with history that is renewed year after year. Although Australia is far away from the Old Continent, on the day of the horse race all distances seem to vanish and the phenomenal history of thoroughbred racing comes together again. Indeed, English thoroughbreds made their way even to Australia and with them came the passion for racing and betting, a passion that has developed into an equestrian reality that has managed to earn significant prominence on the international turf scene. The Melbourne Cup was organized for the first time by the Victoria Racing Club at the Flemington Racecourse on 7 November 1861. The race is now the most important handicap race in the world for horses 3 and older, over a distance of 2 miles (3,200 meters). The choice of a handicap race, i.e., a race in which horses are

220 *At the Melbourne Cup, the stands at the racecourse are bursting with people. It is not so much the passion for racing that grips Australians, but the passion for betting.*

221 *The Flemington track, where all the greatest gallopers in the world have competed. The Melbourne Cup is one of the most famous turf events in the world, as well as one of the few horse races that can attract the attention of an entire nation.*

AUSTRALIA

MELBOURNE

penalized (handicapped) with extra weight that is determined on the basis of their performance results, was adopted in order to render the outcome of the race as uncertain as possible. And it is perhaps for this reason that favorites almost never win. The Melbourne Cup is a very difficult race, and records prove it. For over a century, only two horses had won two editions of the Melbourne Cup: Archer (1861 and 1862) and Peter Pan (1932 and 1934). Only recently, two others joined the club: Rain Lover (1968 and 1969) and Think Big (1974 and 1975). The undisputed champion at the moment, however, is Makybe Diva, winner of three editions (2003, 2004 and 2005). Initially, in addition to the prize money on offer for the Melbourne Cup, there was a prestigious gold watch, which was replaced in 1919 by a handmade gold trophy. As a result, the unique appeal of this world-class event began to attract major sponsors. Since 1997, Emirates Airline became title sponsor, and the name of the race became Emirates Melbourne Cup. In the 2010 edition, the prize money reached the stratospheric amount of $6 million. One thing, however, remains unchanged, and that is its charm, the result of a long history and 150 editions. The incomparable charm of the Melbourne Cup Racing Carnival.

222 *Anacheeva (on the left) was the winner of the 2010 Melbourne Cup. Another mare, Makybe Diva, won the race three times. In the annals of history Makybe Diva is followed by four other gallopers, each winning the race twice.*

222-223 *The Melbourne Cup is a "handicap" race, a feature that always makes the outcome uncertain until the end. It is no coincidence that traditionally the favorites almost never manage to win on the 2 mile race track.*

224 *Originally, a gold watch was awarded to the winner of the Melbourne Cup. This was later replaced by a gold trophy. Thanks to the sponsors, however, the race now has a budget of over $6 million.*

225 *The Melbourne Cup is reserved for Thoroughbreds 3 years and older. These exceptional horses from around the world are the stars of a race that has now reached its 150th edition.*

The Red Coats

CANADA

THE HISTORY OF THE ROYAL CANADIAN MOUNTED POLICE IS ONE OF MANY ACTS OF HEROISM.

Even those who do not know Canada well will have heard of the famous Mounties. Indeed, the adventurous history and heroic deeds of this glorious mounted police force have been featured in literary works and films that have made this epic force known to the whole world, so much so that the Red Coats are one of the symbols of Canada. But the "Mounties" are much more for Canadians because for more than a century they have represented law and order and have been a reliable resource in every situation.

The history of the Red Coats began in 1873, when almost the entire population was still concentrated on the Atlantic coast. The only ones to venture into the rest of the territory, from the Great Lakes to the vast prairies of the West and on to the Rockies, were a few groups of buffalo hunters and unscrupulous smugglers. They had built so-called "trading posts" where they traded alcohol with the Indians and where the only law that existed was the law of the jungle. To re-establish law and order, the Canadian government decided to create a corps of mounted police that would be sent to the West. And this is how, with the enlistment of 318 men, the North West Mounted Police was founded on 23 May, 1873 with a red uniform like that of the British army.

The first heroic undertaking of the Red Coats was the transfer to the territories assigned to them, after a grueling march for horses and riders that left almost one third of the men unhorsed. Nonetheless the Red Coats succeeded in their mission. They divided up the immense territory and founded outposts that were instrumental in ending the trade of adulterated whiskey that was bringing about the destruction of the Blackfoot and Assiniboine Indian tribes. By ensuring the administration of justice, the Red Coats were also able to earn the respect of the Indian leaders with whom they made agreements, establishing the conditions for the construction of the great Trans Canadian Railway and promoting the settlement of colonists, who began to move inland from the coast. In these phases, as in all phases crucial to the history of Canada, the North West Mounted Police always played an impartial role as a guarantor. They did this upon the arrival of Sitting Bull's Sioux Indians from the United States of America and during the frenzied and chaotic gold rush in the Yukon Territory. For their extreme dedication to duty, in 1904 King Edward VII bestowed the title of "Royal" on the North West Mounted Police. In July 1919 the duties of this police force were extended to the whole of Canada. On 1 February, 1920, legislation was implemented establishing the Royal Canadian Mounted Police.

Despite the gradual replacement of horses with mechanized transport, the Royal Canadian Mounted Police have always maintained a mounted group and the historical uniform with the red jacket and the broad-brimmed hat for ceremonial duties. Even today, the performances of the 36 riders who make up the so-called "musical ride", the display team of this police force, maintain the charm of the Red Coat tradition unchanged.

226-227 *THE MOUNTED MILITARY POLICE CORPS DERIVES FROM THE NORTH WEST MOUNTED POLICE, ESTABLISHED IN 1873 ON THE INITIATIVE OF COLONEL PATRICK ROBERTSON-ROSS TO PRESIDE OVER THE PRAIRIES OF WESTERN CANADA. IT IS BASICALLY A CIVILIAN POLICE FORCE, BUT MANY OF ITS MEMBERS SERVED AS VOLUNTEERS IN THE FIRST WORLD WAR.*

227 *AFFECTIONATELY KNOWN AS "MOUNTIES," THE RED COATS HAVE ALWAYS BEEN A SOURCE OF PRIDE FOR THE CANADIAN POPULATION AND, LIKE THE MAPLE LEAF, ARE ONE OF THE COUNTRY'S NATIONAL SYMBOLS.*

CANADA

228 TOP *THE MUSICAL RIDE, THE HORSE DISPLAY THAT IS WELL-KNOWN AND APPRECIATED THROUGHOUT THE WORLD, SHOWCASES THESE RIDERS' SKILLS AND EXCEPTIONAL LEVEL OF TRAINING. THEIR RED UNIFORMS CREATE A STRIKING EFFECT AS THEY EXECUTE THEIR ROUTINES.*

228 BOTTOM *THE COLOR OF THE JACKET CHOSEN WHEN THE CORPS WAS FOUNDED DERIVES FROM THE HISTORIC UNIFORM WORN BY SOLDIERS OF MANY REGIMENTS OF THE BRITISH ARMY, AND THIS IS WHY THE MOUNTIES WERE ALSO CALLED "RED COATS."*

228-229 *THE CORPS INCLUDES A GROUP OF 36 MOUNTED POLICE WHO, IN ADDITION TO CEREMONIAL DUTIES, PERFORM IN THE MUSICAL RIDE.*

CANADA

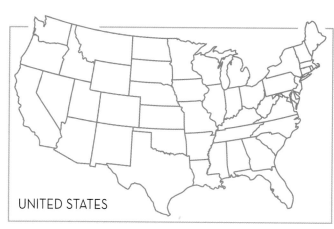

UNITED STATES

Rodeo

CANADA, UNITED STATES

ORIGINATING IN THE CATTLE-TENDING WORKING ENVIRONMENT IN THE FAR WEST, IT HAS BECOME, OVER TIME, A VERY POPULAR SPORT IN NORTH AMERICA.

Technically, the term "Rodeo" means rounding up cattle in a circular enclosure. Rodeo originated with cowboys' traditional daily work but it has now become a popular sport in the United States, and has spread to many other parts of the world, such as Chile, where it has been declared the national sport by the Olympic Committee. There are many different disciplines in a Rodeo, practiced with colts, calves or bulls, but the most famous of them all is Bareback Bronc riding, which involves riding a wild, unbroken horse without a saddle. Cowboys must stay on the horse for 8 endless seconds. Saddle Bronc riding is another discipline where cowboys are also expected to ride the horse for 8 seconds, but with a small saddle and two reins. In bull riding, the rider must remain on the back of a bucking bull for 10 seconds. Rodeos are held both in the United States and in Canada. No village in the West fails to organize a Rodeo for a special occasion. The most famous Rodeos are in Calgary, Canada and in Phoenix, Arizona, where the world Rodeo championship is held every year. A Rodeo champion, in his country of origin, enjoys the same degree of fame and fortune as a premier division soccer player in Europe. In the course of his career, which is limited to a short time span due to the physical effort involved, a professional Rodeo cowboy can make a real fortune, but there is always the risk of ending up

in the hospital and ending his career abruptly. The risk of being unhorsed and trampled by a colt is in fact very high.

Each year in June, modern day "Wild West" cowboys relive the glorious moments of their ancestors in a great event: the Calgary Stampede in Canada. This city is the ideal location for a Rodeo, as it is located in the heart of a region that is full of large ranches, not far from the border with the United States. In Thermopolis in the State of Wyoming, Western saddle equestrian enthusiasts wait impatiently for the month of September to celebrate Ranch Days, a popular festival in which horses are the protagonists. In Bishop, California, every year in May there is a very special Rodeo where mules are the stars of the event and, for a few days, the city becomes "the capital of the mule." These equines take part in the same trials as the horses, in addition to some special ones that have been designed especially for mules. Some tests are reserved for female riders who also ride the mules, especially in barrel racing.

230-231 RODEO DERIVES FROM THE DAILY WORK OF TRADITIONAL COWBOYS. TODAY IT IS A VERY POPULAR SPORT IN THE UNITED STATES AND HAS SPREAD TO MANY OTHER PARTS OF THE WORLD.

231 BAREBACK BRONC RIDING INVOLVES RIDING A WILD, UNBROKEN HORSE WITHOUT A SADDLE AND MANAGING TO STAY ON FOR 8 SECONDS, SOMETHING THAT THIS COWBOY HAS FAILED TO DO.

232-233 *The cowboy grabs the traditional lasso that goes around the horse's neck and hangs on with his hand to stay on horseback during a rodeo exercise.*

233 *This is the moment when horse and rider are closed in the box just before the beginning of their performance: as soon as the door opens, the horse enters the rodeo ring and the trial begins.*

234-235 *Rodeo cowboys always run the risk of being unsaddled and trampled by a colt on the run. Indeed, many professionals are compelled to cut their careers short because of the injuries and the considerable physical effort that are involved in practicing this sport.*

The symbol of the United States of America

UNITED STATES

IT HAS BEEN FUNDAMENTAL IN THE HISTORY
OF NORTH AMERICA AND IS PART OF THE NATIONAL HERITAGE.
AND YET, THE MUSTANG TODAY IS AT RISK OF EXTINCTION.

The Mustang is a wild horse that is the symbol of the United States of America and it epitomizes the spirit of the pioneers. It is a symbol of freedom, independence, pride and courage, qualities that have contributed to consolidate the history of this great nation, and it has always been an integral part of American life, with which it has shared centuries of history. Nevertheless, today the Mustang risks extinction because the great herds that inhabit the grasslands are considered an impediment to the economic development of the country.

Mustangs are the ancestors of all American breeds that exist in American territory, where Arab and Barb horses arrived with the Spanish conquistadors in the 16th century. Together with these animals was the small Portuguese Sorraia pony. Once they landed on the Caribbean islands, they began to proliferate and spread. Subsequently, with the arrival of missionaries - dedicated to the conversion of indigenous peoples but also to the breeding of horses - they began to inhabit the territory in real herds. The native people of the area, the American Indians, were immediately at one with the horses, which soon became their inseparable companions in life and work. With the extermination of Native Americans by Europeans, who wanted to appropriate their land, many horses were captured for the cavalry and large herds were dispersed. The free horses ran wild, giving rise to the Wild Mustang, the epic hero of this land. In 1900 there were about two million horses, but today there are less than 30,000 free-roaming Mustangs. Unfortunately, these horses are the victims of a merciless drive aimed at reducing their numbers, mainly because the large herds reduce the amount of grass available for cattle, whose breeding is an important contribution to the economy of the nation. The Bureau of Land Management was established for this purpose: to control the population of wild horses so that they do not proliferate out of proportion and, at the same time, to protect the species. Mustangs have disappeared from at least six states and now most of them live in Nevada. If the Mustang has survived until today, it is thanks to its strong physique, its tenacity and endurance and its extraordinary intelligence. Fast and agile, it is able to flee at high speed, negotiate any type of rough terrain and confront with confidence any adversity that may present itself.

236 THE LEGENDARY TRIBES OF NATIVE AMERICANS FOUND PERFECT COMPANIONS FOR HUNTING AND WAR IN THE BRAVE AND FAST MUSTANGS. TWO SPLENDID EXAMPLES OF THIS BREED RUN FREE IN THE RED DESERT OF WYOMING.

237 THE HISTORY OF THE FAR WEST WAS WRITTEN BY HORSES. THE WILD MUSTANGS WERE THE MASTERS OF THE LAND IN THE GREAT AMERICAN NATURAL RESERVES. THIS POWERFUL STALLION LIVES IN THE REGION OF THE MCCULLOUGH PEAKS, WYOMING.

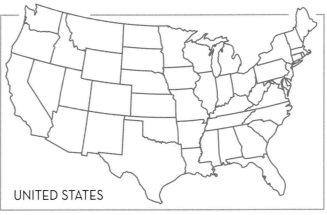

UNITED STATES

238-239 BECAUSE OF THEIR TROUBLED ORIGINS AND A GREAT DEAL OF CROSSBREEDING, MUSTANGS HAVE MANY TYPES OF COATS AND EVEN COATS OF MIXED TYPES. THIS DUN COLOR IS ONE OF THE MOST EASILY RECOGNIZABLE.

239 THE VARIETY OF CROSSBREEDING THAT GAVE RISE TO THESE HORSES IS MANIFESTED IN THE DIVERSITY OF THEIR COATS. A PIEBALD COAT, LIKE THAT OF THIS MARE WITH HER FOAL, IS ONE OF THE MOST COMMON.

240 MUSTANGS ARE PROUD AND WILD HORSES, USED TO DEFENDING THEMSELVES AND FIGHTING FOR SURVIVAL. THEY ARE THE MASTERS OF THEIR TERRITORY AND THEY BREED IN THE WILD. THE HERD IS THEIR REFUGE AND THEIR PROTECTION.

240-241 SINCE HORSES CAN BE PREYED UPON, THESE UNTAMED CREATURES MAINTAIN A STRICT HIERARCHY WITHIN THE PACK THAT ALLOWS THEM TO ORGANIZE REAL GUARD SHIFTS. SOMETIMES THERE ARE FIGHTS AMONG MALES FOR DOMINANCE.

cattle, thanks to their incredible talent with cattle, their famous "cow-sense," still a characteristic of the modern Quarter Horse. Ranch and farm owners stepped up their efforts in horse breeding to obtain strong horses that were of the right height, agile, well balanced, fast and, above all, able to withstand the harsh climate and hard work. Little by little, the breeders grew aware of the need to establish rules and to standardize breeding procedures and, above all, to certify the origins of horses whose records, at the time, were passed down orally.

In 1940, in Texas, the breed took on the official name of Quarter Horse and the American Quarter Horse Association (AQHA) was founded. The first edition of an official show was held in Stamford during the Texas Cowboy Reunion. Since then, the horse of the Far West has taken on an international dimension, becoming one of the most popular horse breeds in the world, with a Stud Book that has gone from around 200 registered horses in 1940 to more than 3 million today. Today, the Quarter Horse is mostly deployed in sports, including competitive ones such as what has now come to be known as Western riding. Endowed with resistance and reliability, the Quarter Horse excels in the Western riding disciplines of reining, cutting, showmanship, Western horsemanship, Western pleasure, trail, Western riding, barrel racing and pole bending. Like its ancestors that worked on farms, herded cattle, transported goods, pulled carriages and spent hours and hours under saddle, the modern Quarter Horse has maintained its characteristics of a multipurpose horse. It is not by chance that the most coveted prize for a breeder is the "All Rounder" prize, which is awarded to the best Quarter Horse that can perform successfully in all disciplines.

244-245 *A COWGIRL CONTROLS A HERD OF HORSES IN THE HARSH COUNTRYSIDE OF THE BADLANDS OF WYOMING IN THE FALL. THIS IS A ROCKY AND RUGGED TERRITORY WITH A WILD LANDSCAPE.*

246 *THE FLEHMEN RESPONSE IS TYPICAL HORSE BEHAVIOR IN RESPONSE TO A SCENT THAT IS VERY DISTINCTIVE; THE HORSE LIFTS ITS HEAD, EXTENDS ITS NECK AND DRAWS BACK ITS LIPS SO THAT IT APPEARS TO BE SMIRKING OR GRIMACING.*

247 *A COLT WITH A BUCKSKIN COAT, A TYPE THAT IS MUCH APPRECIATED BY AMERICAN BREEDERS. THIS COLORING IS CHARACTERIZED BY BLACK LIMBS, MANE AND TAIL, AND ABOVE ALL BY THE LONGITUDINAL DORSAL STRIPE ON THE UPPER BODY.*

248-249 *The Quarter Horse is calm but nonetheless energetic and lively, as this stallion, with a chestnut coat and a particular white ticking on the sides, demonstrates while performing a rodeo-style buck.*

249 *The Quarter Horse has well-developed muscles that sustain its power and speed of movement. It is a horse of striking beauty, as well as being pleasantly disposed toward man.*

250-251 *The Appaloosa owes much of its charm to its spotted coat. Its name comes from the Palouse River, which borders the territory inhabited by the Nez Perce tribe. The "Palouse horse" then became the "Appaloosa Horse".*

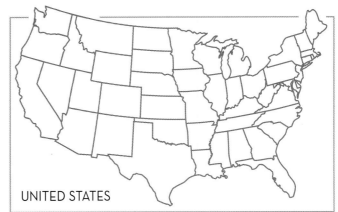

UNITED STATES

The Harlequin of North America

UNITED STATES

IT WAS THE NEZ PERCE TRIBE THAT DEVELOPED THESE EXTRAORDINARY SPOTTED HORSES.

The history of the Appaloosa was written by a people. Indeed, these spotted horses of North America are the result of the passionate work of a proud tribe of Native Americans, the Nez Perce (Pierced Nose). Their encounter probably came about when the horses arrived on the American continent with the Spanish conquistadors.

Indeed, for the Indians, the horse was a completely unknown animal which they called "big dog," not knowing what other animal to compare it with. Their encounter changed the lives of this population and, indeed, together they traveled all over the Great Plains writing the history that turned the tribes of Native Americans into true legends. In the spectacular American films where they were protagonists, the Indians galloped fast and steadily along very narrow trails, where a single horse could barely pass. They went on sheer slopes, river banks and steep mountains where even one false step could lead to their doom, but their horses kept going without hesitation. Thanks to this animal "that is the size of a deer and eats grass," the Indians could easily move their camps. Its speed and agility also allowed the Nez Perce to become skilled hunters. By the early 19th century, they had the largest herd of horses on the continent and were practically the only ones among the Indians of America to practice selective breeding.

The Appaloosa was a source of pride and wealth for the native population as it allowed them to hunt and to move about. It also helped them to trade. The name Appaloosa, however, was coined by the white man.

The territory inhabited by the Nez Perce was bordered by the Palouse River. The horse of this tribe was called "a Palouse horse", a name that later changed to "Palousey," then to "Appaloosey" and finally to "Appaloosa."

This is what the explorer Meriwether Lewis wrote in his diary on February 15, 1806: "Their horses appear to be of an excellent race; lofty, elegantly formed, active and durable. ... Many look like fine English horses. Some of these horses are pied by large spots of white interleaved with black or brown or some other dark color. The greater part, however, are of a uniform color, with markings on their faces and legs and resemble in fleetness and stamina, as well as in shape and color, the best blooded horses of Virginia."

Today, the main and most fascinating feature of the Appaloosa is its spotted coat. There are also so-called "solid" coats or those with no spots, but these are now only a small percentage. The ApHC (Appaloosa Horse Club, founded in 1938 in Idaho) has approved 13 types of pigmentation, with five different types of piebald markings.

From a morphological point of view, the modern Appaloosa is mainly the result of crossbreeding with its compatriot, the Quarter Horse. Besides appearance, the Appaloosa and Quarter share a docile and willing nature. Today the Appaloosa features in all disciplines of American equitation, but it is also an excellent companion for long rides and trekking trips, thanks to its sure-footedness and reliability. Apart from its athletic ability, what makes this animal special are its versatility and reliability. It is an "all rounder", a horse for all seasons.

252 *THANKS TO A GENTLE AND DOCILE NATURE THAT IT SHARES WITH ANOTHER AMERICAN HORSE, THE QUARTER HORSE, THE APPALOOSA FEATURES IN ALL THE DISCIPLINES OF WESTERN RIDING AND IS AN EXCELLENT COMPANION FOR PLEASURE RIDING AND TREKKING.*

253 *THE APPALOOSA HORSE CLUB HAS APPROVED 13 TYPES OF PIGMENTATION, WITH FIVE DIFFERENT TYPES OF PIEBALD MARKINGS. SOME SPECIMENS ARE SPOTTED WITH LARGE WHITE PATCHES INTERSPERSED WITH BLACK OR BROWN, BUT MOST HAVE A SOLID COAT WITH PATCHES ON THEIR FACES AND SOCKS.*

The golden horse

UNITED STATES

THE PALOMINO HORSE'S COAT REFLECTS THE COLOR OF THE SUN
AND IT SHINES LIKE THE GOLD OF A NEWLY MINTED COIN.

Strictly speaking, the Palomino is really not a breed, but a coat color that is particularly common in American horse breeds. A Palomino horse has a glossy coat the color of gold, like that of a freshly minted coin. Its mane and tail are the same color as linen, silver-white. Its skin has dark pigmentation and its eyes are also dark. These are the unique characteristics of a Palomino horse; indeed, there is no breed standard that defines this fascinating horse, but only a well-defined type of coat, which can also be found, for example, in the Quarter Horse and all American breeds of riding horses. These particular horses arrived in America with the Spanish conquistadors. Many of them fled and lived in the wild, mating across breeds and reproducing, giving rise to the different breeds of American horses. Cowboys were fascinated by the golden coat of these horses, a color that they themselves called the "color of the sun." Over time they began to choose the most beautiful individuals, thus starting the selective breeding of the Palomino, a horse that is identified by its coat and not by any particular morphological or attitudinal characteristics as with all true breeds of horses.

The Palomino horse therefore originated in the United States of America, where the American Palomino Horse Association was founded. Today the American Palomino Horse Association is seeking to have the Palomino horse recognized as a breed in its own right. Regarding a Palomino horse's structure, the most common type in the United States is that of the typical American riding horse, such as the Quarter Horse. It is docile, quiet and sturdy, about 155 cm (15.2 hands) high at the withers, and it weighs around 550 kilograms. The golden coat must be of a uniform color; white markings are acceptable only on the face and lower limbs. The Palomino horse is a good riding horse, balanced and willing as well as being very beautiful thanks to its luminous coat. In Britain this type of coat is particularly sought after in sturdy ponies that are suitable mounts for children. Despite efforts in selective breeding, a cross between two Palomino horses does not necessarily produce a third, and that is why it is not possible to define a breed standard.

With their flowing silky manes and tails, Palomino horses are very much appreciated. They display their full splendor in horse shows and in the various disciplines of Western riding competitions, such as the Western pleasure event, in which they are presented with grooming and trappings that highlight their elegance.

255 *IT WAS THE GOLDEN COLOR OF THE PALOMINO THAT MADE IT SUCH A SUCCESS WITH AMERICAN COWBOYS, WHO CROSSED THE MOST BEAUTIFUL HORSES WITH EACH OTHER, GIVING IMPETUS TO THE BREEDING OF HORSES WITH THIS TYPE OF COAT.*

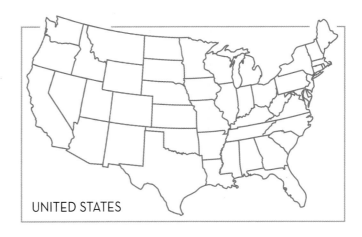

UNITED STATES

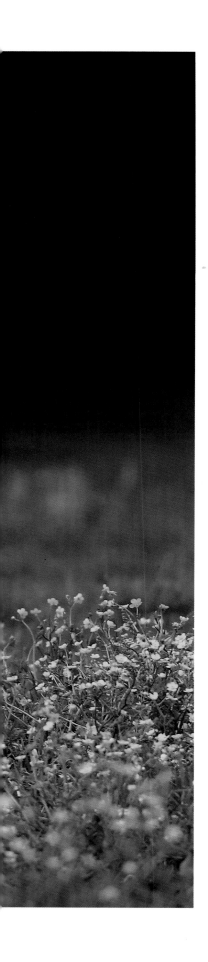

256-257 The elegance of these animals, with their harmonious features, flowing tail and mane and light coat, make them very popular in Western riding festivals and competitions.

257 The white markings of various shapes and sizes are considered acceptable only on the face and lower legs. Thanks to its kind and docile nature as well as its beauty, the Palomino is a great riding horse suitable for both adults and children.

UNITED STATES

A timeless legend

UNITED STATES

MARKINGS OF VARIOUS COLORS, SHAPES AND SIZES MAKE EVERY PAINT HORSE UNIQUE AND COMPLETELY ORIGINAL.

The Paint Horse, the pinto horse, figures in timeless legends and stories that have become international bestsellers which, in turn, have been made into unforgettable films. It is a fascinating animal out of the Old West saga, as well as the undisputed protagonist of the history of its people. Its origins date back to 1519 when the Spanish explorer Hernán Cortés sailed to the American continent in search of fame and fortune. Cortés took horses with him to help his men on their journey across the New World. One of these horses had chestnut and white markings, and it was crossed with the native Mustangs. The result was the American Paint Horse, which is now famous throughout the world. In the early 19th century, the plains of the West were populated by herds of horses, where the original and unique pinto horses thrived. And it is precisely thanks to the colors of their markings and their performance at work that these striking and extraordinary animals became the preferred mounts of the American Indians, the Comanches in particular, who soon became breeders of what is now one of the most popular breeds in the world.

Strong, sturdy and fast, the Paint Horse is an excellent work companion on American ranches; it is skillful with cattle, hardworking and bighearted. Indeed, it is easy to train, docile, intelligent and capable of doing anything. It can run a quarter of a mile faster than a thoroughbred and its ability to sprint is evident in slalom races, weaving around the poles in the pole bending event or around the barrels in barrel racing. It is also excellent when working with calves in rodeo events such as cutting, team penning, roping and working cow, and not least in reining, while its elegance and graceful movements make it ideal for Western pleasure competitions. There is no Western riding discipline in which it does not excel.

Paint Horses are unique because of the markings on their coats. The basic colors are the same as other breeds, but what distinguish the markings are their variety of colors and their shapes. The APHA (American Paint Horse Association) recognizes three marking patterns, Tobiano, Overo and Tovero, which can be distinguished from each other because of their specific characteristics.

258-259 PAINT HORSES EXHIBIT ALL THE POSSIBLE COMBINATIONS BETWEEN WHITE AND THE OTHER COAT COLORS OF A HORSE: BROWN, BLACK, BAY, GRAY, AND SO ON.

258 THIS WIDE RANGE OF COLORS AND MARKINGS CAN BE DIVIDED INTO THREE MAIN VARIETIES: TOBIANO, OVERO AND TOVERO. THE LAST TYPE IS ACTUALLY A CROSS BETWEEN THE FIRST TWO.

259 THE PAINT HORSE HAS A DOCILE AND GENTLE NATURE AND IS EASY TO TRAIN. IT IS HARDWORKING AND HAS A BIG HEART. ITS INTELLIGENCE MAKES IT SUITABLE FOR ANY USE.

260 THANKS TO THEIR PLEASANT APPEARANCE, DUE IN PART TO THE LIVELY
MARKINGS, AND THE FACT THAT THEY ARE HARD WORKERS, THESE HORSES BECAME
THE FAVORITES OF THE TRIBES OF AMERICAN INDIANS, INCLUDING THE COMANCHES,
WHO WERE SKILLED IN SELECTIVE HORSE BREEDING.

260-261 THE PAINT HORSE CAN REACH SPEEDS WELL IN EXCESS OF THAT OF
A THOROUGHBRED. IT EXCELS IN ALL WESTERN DISCIPLINES, AND ITS SPRINT MAKES
IT AGILE AT ALL TIMES.

The conqueror of the Pampas

ARGENTINA ▪ PAMPAS

THE TIRELESS CRIOLLO ACCOMPANIED MAN
IN THE CONQUEST OF THE NEW WORLD.

In the land initially called "Indies," there were no horses. They arrived only with the first landings of the Spanish conquistadors, many of whom followed the route of Christopher Columbus in the 16th century. The horses that were imported from Europe, but above all those developed locally in increasing numbers, spread over the territory as the settlers advanced. These "new" horses were named Criollo, a word that derives from the term "Creole" as used for a person of European descent born in the Spanish, French and Portuguese colonies in Latin America.

To be fully acquainted with the history that led to defining the characteristics of this important breed, we must go back to some key events, such as the conquest of Buenos Aires by the native population. In 1541 Santa María del Buen Aire (as it was called then) was abandoned by the Spanish and almost all of the horses that were there dispersed into the surrounding areas. Once they were free, they found an ideal habitat to which they adapted quickly and easily. Indeed, the vast expanses, in which they began to reproduce, brought about a sort of "miracle," enabling them to quickly recover their primeval instincts and return to being wild horses. Multiplying

continually, these horses produced herds that in a few decades became the undisputed masters of the grasslands of Argentina. Nature, with its laws, took back what had been its own, and the environment of the vast pampas, which has its difficulties with hot summers and cold winters, did the rest, slowly forging the morphology and the exceptional qualities of the Criollo.

Man, however, lost no time in putting the horse back to work. And so he began to catch the wild horses belonging to these herds: after "colonizing" the Pampas, the horse was again either saddled or attached to carts. But it was no longer the animal that had escaped from the conquistadors. Decade after decade spent in the wild had changed it substantially from its Spanish ancestors who lived in captivity. Now, man had before him a horse that was less beautiful and elegant, basically small in stature but very sturdy, with considerable endurance of environmental adversity and remarkably well balanced from a psycho-physical perspective. The Argentinian Criollo was born, a perfect synthesis of the excellent qualities of the Andalusian, Barb and Arab horses of the Spanish, as well as a tough and ruthless natural selection.

The *gauchos* captured the wild horses and retrained them for the different daily uses, and it was they who

263 *THE NAME OF THE CRIOLLO IS DERIVED FROM THE WORD "CREOLE," WHICH USUALLY REFERS TO A PERSON BORN IN LATIN AMERICA OF FRENCH, SPANISH OR PORTUGUESE PARENTS. IN SOUTH AMERICA, HORSES WHOSE ANCESTORS BECAME EXTINCT IN PREHISTORIC TIMES, WERE RE-INTRODUCED BY THE SPANISH CONQUISTADORS.*

PAMPAS

ARGENTINA

worked with the herds to take another decisive step toward the creation of the phenomenal animal that the Criollo would become. Daily hard work did the rest as only the strongest, most efficient, docile, brave and fastest horses were used to herd cattle and, ultimately, could reproduce. The Criollo became the tireless and inseparable companion of the *gaucho* who spent long days on horseback. The *gaucho* and the Criollo were always together in the open air, in the immensity of the pampas, engaged in daily work under the scorching sun or the pouring rain, and a unique symbiotic relationship developed between them. Every day of the year, they depended on each other, and at night they were separated for only a few hours to rest. But it was merely a symbolic separation, because the *gaucho* used the *recado*, i.e., the saddle, as a bed. And it is easy to see what gave rise to that indivisible couple made up of *gaucho* and Criollo - both symbols of pride, courage, honor and above all, love of freedom - which is both one of the emblems of South America and a fundamental element in the development of the Argentinian economy.

264-265 *THE GAUCHOS ARE THE COWBOYS OF THE PAMPAS OF ARGENTINA. DURING THEIR LONG DAYS AT WORK THEY SPEND PRACTICALLY ALL THEIR TIME ON HORSEBACK TENDING TO CATTLE AS THEY HERD THEM FROM RANCH TO RANCH.*

266-267 *HIGHLY SKILLED HORSE TRAINERS, THE GAUCHOS CAPTURED THE WILD HORSES THAT INHABITED THE PRAIRIES AND BROKE THEM IN FOR RIDING AND FOR WORK WITH CATTLE, GIVING RISE TO THE CRIOLLO BREED.*

267 *THE GAUCHOS RIDE EVERY DAY AND IN ALL WEATHER CONDITIONS. THEIR TASK IS TO BREAK IN WILD HORSES, AS WELL AS TO DRIVE THE HERDS OF CATTLE.*

BIOGRAPHIES

SUSANNA COTTICA, was born in Lodi on June 5, 1962. She earned a degree in Modern Foreign Languages and Literature from the Catholic University of the Sacred Heart in Milan, and has been a member of the Italian Association of Professional Journalists as a freelancer since 2001. She is a 3rd level F.I.S.E. (Italian Equestrian Federation) instructor and a rider, particularly in the discipline of show jumping. She is currently an equestrian journalist and writes for the magazines *Cavalli & Cavalieri* and *Il Mio Cavallo*. She completed and edited the Italian translation of *Carnet de Champion* (Ridercom Editions) by French Olympic rider Michel Robert.

LUCA PAPARELLI, was born in Perugia, where he lives and works. He has nearly twenty years of professional journalism experience in the field of equestrian sports and horse breeding, and is an expert on the subject both nationally and internationally. He covers the leading news in horse breeding for *Cavalli & Cavalieri* and *Il Mio Cavallo* magazines, writing articles on athletic and non-athletic horses and reporting on young competitive horses in all equestrian disciplines in Italy and throughout Europe. Among his many diverse activities in the equestrian world, he has been a speaker at the foremost national breeders' events.

INFORMATION

Iceland
Five gaits for a horse
Contact the FEIF (International Federation of Icelandic Horse Associations), website www.feif.org.

Norway
The horses of the Valkyries
An international association based in Norway, the FHI (Fjord Horse International), website www.fjhi.org/, aims to bring together breeding and promotional activities of the various associations around the world.

Ireland
From the land of Eire
For information about the region and the Connemara Pony in particular visit the www.britishconnemaras.co.uk and www.connemara.net websites.

The Precious Piebald
There are various Irish Cob associations. The main one is the Irish Cob Society, based in Ireland, website www.irishcobsociety.com - e-mail info@irishcobsociety.com.

United Kingdom
The smallest in the world
The most important association dedicated to the Shetland Pony is the Shetland Pony Stud-Book Society, which is based in Scotland, website www.shetlandponystudbooksociety.co.uk
- e-mail enquiries@shetlandponystudbooksociety.co.uk.

Germany
Horse Day
For further information about the Rosstag, contact the Tourist Office in Tegernsee: Tegernseer Tal Tourismus GmbH, Hauptstraße 2, 83684 Tegernsee, Germany – Tel. +49-8022-927380 – Fax: +49-8022-9273822 – e-mail info@tegernsee.com. More information is also available on the following sites: www.rottach-egern.de/ and www.tegernsee.com / Veranstaltungen/rosstag.html.

Switzerland
White Turf and Snow Polo
For further information visit the following web sites: www.whiteturf.ch for the White Turf meeting, www.stmoritz-concours.ch for the horse show and www.polostmoritz.com for the polo tournament.

France
The Cadre Noir de Saumur
For further information on the Ecole Nationale d'Equitation et du Cadre Noir and performances, visit the official site: www.cadrenoir.fr.

The horses of the delta
For more information on the Camargue horse, contact the A.E.C.R.C. (Association des Éleveurs de Chevaux de Race Camargue) (Association of Camargue Horse Breeders), website www.aecrc.com (Parc Naturel Régional de Camargue Mas du Pont de Rousty, 13200 Arles - Tel +33- 4-90971925 - Fax +33-4-90971207 - contact@aecrc.com).

Italy
The Blond Mountain horse
Visit the www.haflinger.eu site for more information; for details about the folkloric events refer to www.alta-badia.org/it.

Sa Sartiglia
For further information, contact the Sa Sartiglia nonprofit Social Foundation, website www.sartiglia.info. The headquarters in Oristano are in piazza Eleonora 26, 09170 Oristano – Tel. +39-0783-303159 - e-mail info@sartiglia.info.

Morocco
A distinguished leader
To see the Barbs in Algeria, contact the Stud Farm in Tiaret, website www.haras-tiaret.com.

Mongolia
The wildest in the world
For more information visit the website of the FPPPH (Foundation for the Preservation and Protection of the Przewalski Horse), http://www.treemail.nl/takh/.

United States
Rodeo
For all information on rodeos in the U.S. contact the NPRA (National Professional Rodeo Association), PO Box 212, Mandan, 58554 North Dakota (United States) - Phone +1-701-6634973 - Fax +1-701-6635008 - website: www.npra.com.

From the Far West to the rest of the world
The AQHA (American Quarter Horse Association), which has member associations all over the world, is based in Amarillo, Texas, website www.aqha.com.

The Harlequin of North America
To learn more, visit the ApHC (Appaloosa Horse Club) web site (www.appaloosa.com).

INDEX

PHOTO CREDITS

Cover:
A Lusitano Horse - © Juniors Bildarchiv/Photolibrary.com

WS White Star Publishers® is a registered trademark
property of De Agostini Libri S.p.A.

© 2012, 2014 De Agostini Libri S.p.A.
Via G. da Verrazano, 15 - 28100 Novara, Italy
www.whitestar.it - www.deagostini.it

Translation: Catherine Howard
Editing: Suzanne Smither

Revised edition

ISBN 978-88-544-0931-6
1 2 3 4 5 6   18 17 16 15 14

Printed in China